Call For News
Reflections of a Missionary Pilot

James Rush Manley

Reader Comments

PIREP's of faith. Anecdotes, observations, and humor about how God works in the daily lives of MAF pilots and personnel.
—Dr. H. Pat Arti, Former Naval Aviator, Private Pilot, Founder and President of Performance Associates, Inc.

Jim is a master with words. These every day stories of encounters with God give we who struggle with the messiness of life a God perspective. A must read for pilgrims and priests who want to know and experience God in a deeper way.

Over the years I have been encouraged and inspired by Jim Manley's Call For News column. We are blessed that these treasures of God's truth and wisdom are now in one book. Jim shows us that God's story is really our story lived out every day in cockpit and kitchen.
—Bernie May, Retired missionary pilot, former President of JAARS, former President of Wycliffe Bible Translators, and founder of The Seed Company

The provocative titles in this unique book give glimpses of God's work going on all over the world, day after day through members and staff of Mission Aviation Fellowship. Jim has been there. He knows all about weather, maintenance details, understanding people, understanding language and cultural situations, trying to get along together as Christians are supposed to do. And he writes about it with candor and clarity.

Jim doesn't pretend to be a super saint and he knows his colleagues aren't either. But they all have the same God and come together to pray for one another and be encouraged as the result of these vignettes. Read Plunging the Depth, Grasping Trust, and Hard Places and you'll resonate with Jim's heart. More than that, you'll be blessed, challenged and encouraged. I was. I am.
—Dr. Laura Mae Gardner, Long-time Wycliffe missionary and member of MAF's Board of Directors

Following 17 years as an MAF pilot in Ecuador, Jim Manley was given a new assignment. He was asked to use his writing skills to invite colleagues to share stories of God at work in their lives and among the Indigenous people groups they serve. Readers of this collection of brief essays drawn from his own experiences will be fascinated, amazed, surprised, entertained, and blessed by accounts that illustrate the multifaceted graces of God, and will find themselves pondering at length the thought-provoking questions at the close of each entry.

—Clarie Mellis, Wife of former MAF President, Charlie Mellis

"Call for News-Reflections of a Missionary Pilot by author James Rush Manley is an easy to read devotional book full of humor and anecdotes. It's about how God works in the hearts of pilots and the workforce. The structure and organization is well written. It is filled with Scriptures and the references are located at the end of each vignette making it easy for the reader to do their own research. Each page has a question at the end to help the reader grow personally".

"Mr. Manley has a passion for writing this book stating: 'Tell me, what compels you so strongly that, even when you're fed up with problems, discouraged by disappointments, and have no energy to care anymore, you rise up and do it all over again'. Both his voice and writing style are noteworthy".

—Judge, 23rd Annual Writer's Digest Self-Published Book Awards 2015

DEDICATION

Mission Aviation Fellowship

They graciously allowed me to fly their airplanes to serve
God's people in Earth's forgotten corners.

I received far more than I gave.

CONTENTS

ACKNOWLEDGMENTS

This small book conceals large investments of encouragement, patience and trust. I fear that as I start naming those who helped, I'll miss someone. But I must try.

First, I want to thank my wife, Regina, who continually points me back to Jesus. Because of her, I'm becoming a better person than I am.

Then grateful thanks go to MAF's leaders who trusted me with quarter-million dollar airplanes. Then they allowed me five years in the bully pulpit as editor of *Around the World* and creator of *Call For News*.

My friend, Donna Burns, first helped me see the Lord's timing years before a single word appeared on paper. My marvelously merciless, writing mentor, Neva Coyle, demanded only the best. Bernie May first suggested collecting the Call For News columns into a book. Larrie Gartner and Alan Lindvall continually encouraged me. Bob Fish frequently used my columns as a devotional with the hangar crew. Many others around the world who took the time to share how these columns blessed them, convinced me that if I let Him, the Holy Spirit would speak.

Finally I have to thank hundreds of people – MAF staff, our prayer and financial supporters, Ecuador's Latino and Indigenous people, as well as the missionaries we worked with. Jesus spoke through each of them to reveal Himself. They provided the seeds that grew into these stories.

FOREWORD

This book is dedicated to MAF and its wonderful people but … it's all about Jesus!

Over the past twenty years or so I have read dozens of books and articles that inspired. This book reminds us so clearly Who our bedrock is. The stories, some drawn from Jim's experience as an MAF aviator and some are just life, abound with invaluable inspiration and challenge in the most poignant way.

Our planes carry people to where they want to go, while our people move those we serve towards Jesus. Our planes fly high enough to clear all physical obstacles, while our people demonstrate viewing life from heaven's perspective.

Jesus provides simple ways for us to follow Him on our "flight" through our time on this earth. MAF's people do this every day in very difficult situations by remembering two things: hold heading and maintain altitude.

Jim's conviction that God continually speaks to all of us yields 'pearls' of examples in the following pages. Each story's final question, many beginning with "So, what happened when …" leave us in no doubt that we are driven to look and listen for the wonderfully custom tailored way Jesus cuts through the clutter, noise and mess of life to reach out to us.

The apostle Paul recognized the importance of the Christian life as a day-by-day process when he wrote: "I do not consider myself yet to have taken hold of it. But one thing I do: Forgetting what is behind and straining toward what is ahead, I press on toward the goal to win the prize for which God has called me heavenward in Christ Jesus" (Philippians 3:13-14) So, hold heading and maintain altitude. If your progress seems a little slow just remember: Patience! God is not finished with us yet!

May your life be enriched as you read this gem of a book.

John Boyd, President & CEO Mission Aviation Fellowship

PREFACE

God wired me with two professional passions – flying and writing. Mission Aviation Fellowship (MAF) sent me to Ecuador, where I served six people groups, speaking five different languages. I flew Cessna 185s and 206s in the Andes Mountains and both the Coastal and Amazon Jungles. Concurrently, I also worked as a radio technician and, for the final six years, as the program manager.

The indigenous jungle people taught me that obscure languages and strange cultures cover similar hearts. At our core, we all want pretty much the same thing. But communicating heart-hopes across those barriers challenges skill and threatens identity. That's when I realized what my drive to write was all about—translating the little bit of heaven's music I could hear into people-speak.

Regina and I raised four kids in Ecuador, worked crazy hours, ate weird things, made many friends and, when I could, I wrote. After 17 years, the Ecuador chapter closed and I transferred to our support staff in the U.S., where I started writing copy for our Development department. Not exactly the great American novel, but word-crafting nonetheless.

One afternoon my boss leaned into my "Dilbert©" cubicle and asked if I'd take over editing our weekly, in-house Ezine, _Around The World_ (ATW). I nodded and said, "ah … sure." As any editor will tell you, to publish regularly, you must have a constant stream of material to work with. So every Tuesday I sent an email reminder to our staff around the world asking for relevant personal and ministry news. The subject line always read, _"Call for News."_

If I reminded our staff, I had plenty to work with. If I forgot they forgot, and Thursday's ATW edition would look very slim. While the reminder's value proved clear, it also proved boring. After all, how many different ways could I say, "Send me your news"?

One Tuesday, while harassing hard working folks to let the rest of us in on their lives, I put myself back into the cockpit. Instead of a keyboard at my fingertips, I held fists full of yoke and throttle. The sound, smell, sight and motion rushed in. And the thoughts – mine and the Lord's—welled up. My feeble questions, my whining, what I wondered, what I observed, what I learned, what I still chaffed over, mistakes, victories, swimming in His grace—all of it started flowing from some forgotten heart chamber through my brain and into my fingers. I rarely experienced fear while flying. But my strongest memory, while hanging by one propeller and four wing attach-bolts over that vast jungle, was that Jesus was always very, very close. That's where my running conversation with Him grew from trickle to torrent.

I wasn't anybody special, so I knew that God had to be talking to all of our staff regardless of the backwater hollow they'd been assigned to. I got excited. If I'd been having such a great time with the Lord, how cool would it be to hear what He was doing with all of us? I really wanted to know, "What's God saying to you? What's He doing through you, around you, with you?" So, I started calling for the news, the really good news I knew was out there.

This book compiles the best of nearly five years asking, from different angles, the same basic question every week. I received such amazing answers that I knew there had to be more. So, now it's your turn. There's no doubt He's working around you, like rain on the just and the unjust. The trick to seeing is asking. And that's a question our Daddy loves to answer.

James Rush Manley Meridian, Idaho May 2010

PREFACE TO THIRD EDITION

God's Word remains timeless. He continues to inundate us with his song of wisdom, direction, creation, and love. We can partake anytime if we'll stop, look, and listen. My prayer is still that you will see and hear him at work around you, and then incline your heart to respond. He offers us a wild, exciting ride that is so worth the terrifying delight of unexpected joy.

And, as we sold out the last of the second edition's copies, I realized this third edition should include both print and electronic versions. You'll find both available.

James Rush Manley Meridian, Idaho July 2018

Using This Book

One size does not fit all

Some of these stories will speak to you the first time you read them. Others won't. Ask the Holy Spirit what He has specifically for you. Go at your own pace – one a day, one a week, or whenever He leads you on to the next one.

Read a story, then meditate on just one or two of the references

The verses listed touch ideas in each story, but are not the only ones that apply, nor even the "best" ones. Instead, they provide a starting point of what He says about a subject. When you read the story again at another time, choose a different reference.

Most scripture references tell many stories

I repeat some scripture references because God's Word is bigger on the inside than the outside. The deeper we go, the more expansive it becomes. But that shouldn't surprise us. After all, "In the beginning was the Word, and the Word was with God, and the Word was God." And, "Of the increase of His government and peace there will be no end."

Isaiah 9:7   John 1:1

JAMES RUSH MANLEY

1. If You Can?

The candidates [potential MAF missionaries] arrived today, wide-eyed and willing to believe anything we tell them. But we know that after a few months struggling with bad weather, civil disturbances, poor communications, cross-cultural frustration, lost mail, and a leaky cylinder, their sharp belief will take on a fuzzy edge. Embarrassing feelings will pop up from beneath the swamp of weariness and frustration as they struggle to keep the faith.

A desperate father once cried out to Jesus, "… if you can do anything, take pity on us and help us."

Jesus replied, "'If you can?' Everything is possible for him who believes."

The honest father exclaimed, "I do believe; help me overcome my unbelief!" When we confess the truth, the Lord carries us, while, at the same time, demanding deeper faith.

While He's holding your program together, what gauntlet of impossible belief has He thrown down before you?

Jeremiah 33:3   1 John 1:9   Mark 9:14-29   Ephesians 3:20-21

1

2. Motley Crew Glue

Have you ever wondered about the Body of Christ? What did God have in mind when He put together this motley crew of brigands? We have as many opinions about what He wants as there are members. Some days, we not only have trouble rowing together, we can't even agree that we're in a boat. Why does He risk His name on such a ship of fools?

Part of the answer has to be love. Paul says that as we speak the truth, we will "grow up into Him who is the Head, that is, Christ." He goes on to say that "From Him the whole body, joined and held together by every supporting ligament, grows and builds itself up in love, as each part does its work." His love squishes out from the seams of our work like magic glue. It transforms a band of pirates into a company of saints.

So, how is He using your work to stick His body together?

Romans 12:3-8   Ephesians 4:14-16

3. Visible Heart

At Oshkosh [the world's largest air show held annually in Oshkosh, Wisconsin] last night, an MAF recruiter told the story of a national preacher speaking to a church in the US. The preacher held up one arm saying, "These are the prayers of all of you rising up to the throne of God." Then he raised the other, meeting the first high over his head and said, "And these are the prayers of the believers in my country rising up to that same throne. Though only a few of us have met here on Earth, we already know each other in the Lord."

Our clients live in strange cultures. We don't understand them. They think we're weird and often miss what we try to share. Yet, all believers are citizens of the same country. His culture is the standard—not ours or theirs. Heart meets heart in His throne room.

So, how is He allowing a client to see your heart?

Ephesians 2:19-20   Philippians 3:17-21

4. Adjusted Perspective

The night sky adjusts our perspective. Vast distance separates us from the stars we see. If we could fly at the speed of light (just shy of 670 million mph) it would take us 775 years to get to Rigel, the hot blue star that marks the lower right corner of Orion. An airliner could make the trip in 902 million years, while a Cessna 206 would take a bit longer—3.7 billion years, not counting downtime for maintenance.

On a practical basis, we can gaze, we can long, and we can wish, but we can't cross. The good news is that while the stars may be unreachable, it turns out that they're not untouchable. They send us a steady stream of photons that our retinas detect as light. Whether we open our eyes or not, we're awash in a continual cascade of star stuff.

An un-crossable gulf separates us from God. On a practical basis, we can't cross it, nor could we even if we were granted all of time. Fortunately, He takes the initiative to reach us. His presence touches everything and everyone at all times. Even if we can't see Him, He pours Himself out on the just and the unjust. The problem is that our retinas aren't designed to detect His Spirit. Our hearts are. A grieving hymn writer understood when he pleaded, "Lord, haste the day when my faith shall be sight ..."

So, how is faith opening glimpses of Heaven where you are?

**Matthew 5:45   Exodus 23:20   Acts 17:27-28   John 5:37
Jeremiah 23:24**

5. The Deal

When we first acknowledged Jesus as Lord, most of us secretly thought, "He's getting a pretty good deal." Oh sure, we were in a jam and needed help, but we pictured ourselves as valuable assets to His Kingdom. We saw it as the classic win/win swap—a fair exchange where both parties bring something valuable to trade.

The truth is we brought nothing; He brought everything. We gave him all of our junk: lust, envy, idolatry, hatred, and rebellion. He, on the other hand, gave us an easy burden and a light yoke; new life, victory over sin, darkness flees at our word, death is defanged, and we get to spend forever ruling and reigning with Him. Then, as if that weren't lopsided enough, He added, "Cast all your cares on me."

It was never meant to be a fair deal, because it was never a deal at all. It was meant to reveal that apart from Him, we can do nothing. But it also reveals that we can do all things through Christ Jesus who strengthens us.

So, what's He doing through you?

1 Peter 5:7   Philippians 4:10-13   John 15:1-8

6. The Trump Card

We believers know to do God's will—that's the easy part. But why should we? Because He loves us, or we love Him? Or maybe because He made the universe and knows better than anybody how it works? Or perhaps because He can zap us into cinders if we don't? All true, but He's concerned with our hearts.

Actions are important, but motivation trumps doing. And that's the hard part. Rules are easy; motives are obscure. The human heart is desperately wicked, who can know it?

Fortunately, He does. He weighs every motive, every thought, every intent. Picking His way doesn't come from mindless response. He didn't endure the cross to create an army of robots. Instead, He demonstrates the difference between doing His will for ourselves and doing His will for Him by posing the question: "Who gets the glory, you or me?" Then, He steps back while we choose.

So, what choices do you face?

Jeremiah 17:9   Matthew 6:21   1 Samuel 15:22   1 Corinthians 10:31 Proverbs 16:2

7. Working Grace

Grace, a lovely name picked for cherished daughters by parents hoping to impart gentle softness. And we call some graceful because they move not only with coordination, but also harmony and rhythm. When we speak of the Lord's grace, we often envision sunlight on roses under a willow tree—all good and true, but incomplete.

Jesus threw us a rope while we wallowed in a sewer. He pulled us out, slimy and putrid, a dripping mass of   . well, you know. Then, after He cleaned us, He said each one of us should use whatever gift we have received to serve others, faithfully administering God's grace in its various forms. What forms does His grace take?

How about throwing 3,600 pounds of aluminum at a mud hole you wouldn't drive your car on, hoping someone there will reach out for God's rope? Or herding obstinate electrons down a radio's long, skinny wires. Or wrestling an aluminum rivet until it holds two pieces of sheet metal together. Or spinning old bruised vegetables into a golden feast. Or chasing elusive numbers through stacks of legers until they play nice and agree with other numbers.

His grace is altogether lovely, but it's also strong and willing to get dirty. So, how is He asking you to administer His grace?

1 Peter 4:7-11   Romans 3:21-26

8. Reality Test

Some psychology courses recommend we don't challenge delusions—fixed, false beliefs that are resistant to reason or confrontation with actual fact. But who consistently holds lies so close that the lie becomes reality? Who creates their own parallel world invisible to others but granite-hard to the keeper? Is this the exclusive domain of crazies, or do we all cling to some distorted imitation of facts? Do we cherish resentment? Do we choose anxiety? Do we wallow in greed or bask in superiority?

Jesus is the truth—not a truth, or the greatest truth, but the one and only truth. We measure the realness of everything else by how much it looks like Him, like what He says, like what He creates. He confronts our shadowy labyrinths, challenges us to defy our own nature, and pleads with us to agree with Him. Repentance is when we do. Sin is when we don't.

So, how is He using you to reconcile your worlds—internal and external—to His Kingdom?

John 1:1-5   John 3:16-21   John 1:14   John 14:6

9. Hidden Motivation

A maximum-weight takeoff from a 300-meter, muddy airstrip can reveal that the shiny airplane hides poor rigging and a weak cylinder. But professional aviators know that a successful flight operation depends upon good maintenance, so we inspect our machines thoroughly. The veracity of our internal procedures determines if we accomplish our mission or not. Order parts on time, or the airplanes don't fly. Balance the checking account, or run out of money. So, we reconcile carefully.

However, hard work to tame hidden things has a drawback—no splash, no glory, no praise. Who sees our efforts? The Lord for sure, but what about everybody else? Do they see? Do they care? Outsiders neither understand nor appreciate our labor. So sometimes we consider fudging a bit, bypassing the hidden stuff and going for the stage. After all, the show must go on. Fortunately, we usually resist the lie.

The problem is, of course, that even after fierce battles, visible flame still draws us like beguiled moths. We forget that judging the outside without knowing the inside produces wrong conclusions.

So, how is His still, small voice showing up in the hidden jobs and unknown people of your ministry?

1 Kings 19:11-13   Matthew 6:5-6   1 Chronicles 28:9

10. Culture's Coat

A picture shows an MAF plane and pilot on a jungle airstrip. He stands in a large circle of praying adults. Older kids look about; younger ones sit naked in the grass, clustered near the middle. Differences reveal location. The black people stand straighter than the brown of South America where I served. A generic Cessna 206 sits in the grass. But the propeller blades taper to the thin point of a normally aspirated engine rather than the wide, squared-off tips of the turbocharged model we used in the Andes Mountains. So, this guy flies mostly into lower elevation airstrips. Ah yes, the pilot. I recognize him. That confirms my guess. The differences say these folks live in eastern Africa.

Differences, indeed. This impromptu prayer meeting took place on the other side of the planet. But they train us to deal with differences. We tread lightly, constantly worrying that a stupid, cultural blunder will ruin a generation's missionary effort. Will the dictionary's translation endear us or mark us as uncouth louts? How do we shake hands? Are men allowed to speak to women? Can women speak to anybody? Do we say no to the extra 50 pounds of cargo directly, or start by saying yes? Is telling the truth important or a joke everyone smirks about? Does each life have equal value or does power give worth? The labyrinth defies navigation.

On the other hand, a 206—turbo or not—is still a Cessna. The Ituri Forest looks identical to the Amazon Jungle. Chiggers bite at all grass airstrips. Paul said that all men, everywhere, ought to pray. In how many corners of the world do we circle for prayer? We serve the same Lord, belong to the same Body, and claim citizenship in the same Kingdom. Culture's coat only hides man's spirit, it does not extinguish it. Underneath, we all have hopes, dreams, fears and needs. Jesus redeemed all of us alike—Dong Chinese, Shuar headhunters, Nebraska housewives, and Laplanders. We can learn to live outside of our culture, but seeing others outside of theirs defies us. Still, we can do all things through Him who strengthens us.

So, how does He reveal His design to you in others?

Romans 10:12   2 Corinthians 5:16-21   1 Corinthians 12

11. Contradictions

Contradictions obscure what ought to be clear. God promises to open closed doors—just ask, seek, and knock. He commands, "Be strong and courageous." He says the devil will flee if we resist. And if we like, go ahead and move that offending mountain. Clear directions speak to the point, and fit goal-oriented theology.

But He confuses everything. He told the folks on a hillside to turn the other cheek and give to him who asks. And He says we're supposed to wait. Wait for what? How do meek saints inherit the Earth while taking the Kingdom by force? How can we do what He wants when knowing what He wants eludes us? Yes, we believe Him. But sometimes it seems we need a Captain Midnight Secret Decoder Ring to crack the cipher. Turn the dial, match the letters, and voilà! The hidden message appears.

On the other hand, how does an infinite, eternal God communicate with creatures confined to space and time? Try discussing morality with your kid's hamster. Stick your fingers into the cage, perhaps, but true understanding will evade you. Impossible? Of course. But He delights making rivers in our deserts. He safeguarded this mystery's key in His rest. When we return to "wait," when we submit—not hide—our passions, we surpass one who takes a city. Only then can we hear the still, small voice of the Counselor making everything plain.

So, what impossible obstacle lounges insolently between you and what He commands?

Isaiah 40:29-31   Matthew 7:7-12   Isaiah 64:4
Matthew 11:28-30   Proverbs 16:32   Matthew 21:21-22
Matthew 5:38-42   James 4:7

12. Deceitful Heart

Jerusalem's ashes cooled. Lizards crawled among the stones. But the dreams returned every night—Babylonian spears, Babylonian swords, first red then dried to crusty brown, yet still hungry. Now daylight brought more. King Nebuchadnezzar left Gedaliah in charge of the remnant. Then Ishmael killed him, captured all the Jews, and forced them across the desert. But Johanan rescued everyone. Wide, bulging eyes darted back and forth. "We can't stay here. The king of Babylon will kill the rest of us when he finds out what happened. Run! Hide! Hide in Egypt!"

Johanan and his officers pleaded with Jeremiah to inquire of the Lord. "Where should we go? What should we do? Tell us and we will obey the Lord our God."

Jeremiah said, "Okay, I'll ask God and tell you everything He says." Ten days later he called them together. "God says you should stay here. If you do, everything will be fine. However, if you go to Egypt, what you fear will catch up with you."

Nightmares flashed just behind their eyes. "No! You're lying! God didn't say that! You're against us! Run to Egypt! We'll be safe there." And so they fled and died. How could they do that after generations of foretelling came to pass before their eyes?

Today, we call such people fools, and the more cautious among us remember to watch our step. But the broken plead for mercy when they look into the rubble and recall that "the heart is deceitful above all things and beyond cure. Who can understand it?"

So, how has the Lord granted you His unmerited favor recently?

Jeremiah 17:9   Luke 18:9-14   Jeremiah 41:1– 43:7

13. Incomplete Counterfeits

One day, religious leaders challenged Jesus when the people worshiped him. He didn't lower his gaze, furrow his brow with a half-smile, or give a bemused headshake saying, "No, no, no, their enthusiasm carries them to excess." Instead he looked the question in the eye and said the rocks would praise him if men did not. He agreed that he was Lord and master. He proclaimed himself the Father's Son and source of true food and drink. He claimed to be God, the Creator of the universe. Yet, the same Spirit also says he wouldn't break a reed and names him the humble standard to follow.

With us, however, condemnation mimics humility. The voice in our head says we are not smart enough, tall enough, pretty enough, skinny enough, spiritual enough, strong enough, lucky enough, clever enough, rich enough, a good enough pilot, good enough mom, good enough wife, good enough husband, good enough lover, good enough missionary, whatever. The enemy's tape plays the mantra over and over until we call it truth.

Fortunately, counterfeits present incomplete truth. God's Word does call us unworthy, unrighteous, and doomed for destruction. But condemnation's lie stops us there. Running from arrogance, we don't recognize the inside-out sock of selfishness and call it humility instead. We forget that He chose us in Him before the creation of the world to be holy and blameless in His sight. The whole truth adds that, while apart from Him we can do nothing, we can, in fact, do all things through Christ who strengthens us. Christ alone changes cracked pots into fountains of living water.

So, how are His blessings flowing out of you to those around you?

**Matthew 16:16-17　John 8:58　Luke 19:37-40　John 13:13
John 6:55　Ephesians 1:3-10**

14. True Light

My shoes squished with every step. A shiny trail ran between my desk and a dripping umbrella waiting by the door for my next trip across the ramp. Six weeks of rain and mottled gray sky made it hard to remember any other color existed. I was tired—tired of wet feet, parked airplanes, and a waiting room full of people who only wanted to go home. Occasionally, the ceiling lifted just enough to fly, so we'd try to do a week's work in two or three hours. A mad, splashing scramble to load passengers and cargo, and then a parade of planes trundled to the end of the runway. The high humidity formed misty condensation halos around spinning propellers. The bark of supersonic propeller tips momentarily pulsed over roaring engines as each plane took off.

If all this hustle worked, the planes came back in a couple of hours coated with weedy, slimy mud. Often, though, it ended in frustration when the jungle strips were too wet to land on or the ceiling dropped back down to the trees. Then, the whole idea of ministry sank into a sloppy bog. Life degenerated to a dull sea of catching up on old jobs, washed over by waves of apathy. Sure, there was finally more time, but it was hard to read, hard to plan, hard to pray, hard to believe.

But then, I'd make an emergency flight to Quito. The official instrument procedure dictated a climb to the east over the jungle up to 10,000 feet before turning back west for the mountains. I had to make 15,000 feet by the entrance to the pass. The featureless gray outside gave no clues of earth, sky, or motion. Life became simple. Follow the instruments and live, or ignore them and die. Then, ever so slowly, the gray wet wrapping brightened. Suddenly it broke to blinding, cobalt blue above and rolling hills of dazzling white below. True light shone everywhere with exuberance and wild generosity. Dark, moldy, tendrils clinging from the foggy depths below vanished like a bad dream forgotten. The sun shone whether I could see it or not, and the cloud color depended entirely upon which side I looked at.

So, which side of life faces you these days?

**Job 42:5   John 14:19   2 Kings 6:17   Romans 8:28-30
Isaiah 33:15-17**

15. Blind Eyes Behold

We believe God's promises, yet even on our best days a shallow scratch reveals festering discontent. Disappointed, we see less than we expect. One voice in our head whines, "We play His game, so He owes us, right? Success, health, happiness, some sort of payment for our good deeds." Another confesses along with the Psalmist, "Lord, you have assigned me my portion and my cup; you have made my lot secure. The boundary lines have fallen for me in pleasant places; surely I have a delightful inheritance."

We struggle because fickle eyes make it hard to recognize God's blessings. If we desire to see Him, even blind eyes behold oceans of grace, stretching farther than sight and horizon, beyond imagination. But if we desire something else, that's all we see. The Spirit said through Isaiah, "Remember the former things, those of long ago; I am God, and there is no other; I am God, and there is none like me." Like salvation, faith precedes experience and belief comes before sight.

So, how do you see the Lord's kindness around you?

**Psalm 16:5-6   Mark 16:16   Isaiah 46:9   Luke 1:45
Matthew 21:22   John 6:28-29**

16. Plunging the Depth

We flee suffering, yet it crashes life's party anyway. It drops like an anvil on the cake, messes up the treats and decorations we arranged just so, smashes the table, goes through the floor and gouges into the foundation. It plummets past rational thought, bypasses understanding, ignores defenses and even transcends culture. Suffering's collision with soul's bedrock reveals character like a bell displays its quality with clear tone or dull thud. We can't fake it. Our real nature lies exposed for all to see. We ask "Why?" Then we rail against the gross violation of our rights and demand "Why me?" As if someone else deserves it more. Only He knows the whole story, but we can see at least three small pieces of the mystery.

First, He designed His body to build itself up in love. "God ... comforts us in all our troubles, so that we can comfort those in any trouble with the comfort we ourselves have received from God." Wayward kids pierce our hearts with hot needles of regret and condemnation. A hundred times crying out "Why?" equips us to comfort those still tasting their first tears.

Second, intense suffering strips control and humiliates us. But as Paul said, "... I am not ashamed, because I know whom I have believed, and am convinced that He is able to guard what I have entrusted to Him for that day." He grows us up into Him from the ashes of failed tests. The Judge pronounces us guilty then redeems and refines us into His image.

Third, He inducts us into the "fellowship of sharing in his sufferings." When we fall into the pit of dark terror, we find Him waiting, ready to travel the whole journey with us. Those chosen to walk there tell us that the songs of struck hearts harmonize with His, creating music the rest of us won't hear until He returns. We never seek it, yet we've all touched the waters of that sea—most with damp toes, but some plunge the depth.

So, how did He prepare you and yours to comfort the people you serve?

**2 Corinthians 1:3-7   Philippians 3:7-11   Ephesians 4:14-16
2 Timothy 1:12**

17. Grasping Trust

Slick leather sandals slipped on slimy mud. David's knee struck the cave floor, but he bit his tongue. The other men pressed close in the dark, listening for pursuit. They waited, silent for a long time except for tight, panting breath. Finally, he commanded, Abishai, Ethan, check the way—carefully." The two scouts nodded, turned, and disappeared around a corner more felt than seen.

"Joab, tell them we spend the night here," he said. Then, forcing a straight step, he added, "I'll be back." Taking a newly lit torch, he climbed farther in. Joab's eyes followed a moment. "Off to talk to his God again, I suppose," he muttered to himself then shrugged and moved towards the others.

The pain in David's knee no longer brought tears, but he still limped. When he knew he was alone, he cried out, "Lord, this isn't a kingdom, it's a joke. We have no food, no home. Our families are scattered, and we live like bandits, running from Saul and his army. Why have you deserted us?" Later, he wrote about hiding in that cave, "I cry aloud to the Lord; I lift up my voice to the Lord for mercy. I pour out my complaint before him; before him I tell my trouble." Why did the same God who tells us not to worry also call a complaining David a man after his own heart?

Worry abandons trust and seizes control. Then it offers polite prayers that have nothing to do with heart thoughts. Complaints, on the other hand, cling to trust in the God who commanded, "Cast all your anxiety on him because he cares for you." That passionate honesty confesses reality before the God of truth. Reality may be messy, but that's where God meets us.

So, in what sort of mess is Jesus meeting you these days?

1 Samuel 24:1-4   1 Peter 5:6-7   Psalm 142:1-7

18. Andres

The storm drifted across the jungle, collided with the shrouded Andes Mountains, and dissolved into mist. My calendar said December, but it was hardly a Christmas setting. The vast, dripping Amazon stole all but memory of hot apple cider, sharp stars piercing winter night, and stamping frozen toes while caroling.

My friend, Andres Mashient, on the other hand, looked forward to a Christmas feast of fresh papaya, warm chicha, smoked fish, roasted monkey, and a banana leaf full of steamed yucca. He saw snow as the white peak of a distant volcano, and his people used only three musical notes. No, the rain-forest native didn't know a thing about my Christmas.

But the God of the universe knew his name and where he lived. Jesus called Andres home that mid-December day from inside one of our planes rushing him to the hospital. Now, he gets to play in the Christmas we see only dimly. That really shouldn't be a surprise, though. After all, God called Mary by name, and she got to raise Him. The really good news is that He knows our name, too.

So, where do you hear Him calling you?

1 Kings 22:34-38   2 Timothy 1:8-10   Luke 1:26-28   Revelation 2:17

19. Coexistence

Stick to it. Don't give up. Never surrender. Inspiration's words sound good for fights and messy trials. But to what, exactly, do we stick? The high goals defend the charge of stupidity easily enough—stand to the last man, repelling the invader. Or stay in the fire to rescue the doomed child. But what about living in politically crazed nowhere-bovia when safety's country sits only a choice away? Why raise your children in diseased jungle obscurity when clean opportunity waits at the other end of an airline route? What answer comforts a slandered heart whose faith is labeled obstinate and blind?

What, in fact, distinguishes perseverance from stubbornness? Stubbornness clutches its throne and cries, "My way or the highway!" Perseverance, on the other hand, surrenders its throne. Stubbornness glorifies me. Perseverance glorifies Him. Stubbornness follows its own devices. Perseverance waits for His. Stubbornness controls. Perseverance yields. Stubbornness craves dominion, but love always perseveres.

Stubbornness and perseverance cannot co-exist. Forcing them to live together only makes a double-minded heart. Fortunately, retaining the very smallest of seeds, despite storms and naysayers, produces the largest crop.

So, what's sprouting in *your* garden?

**Luke 11:7-10   Acts 7:51-53   Matthew 10:22   Mark 4:30-32
Luke 5:36-39   2 Corinthians 6:14-18   James 1:2-8**

20. Knowledge

The pilot finally had his chance. The fresh brake pads on the C-185 needed a "burn in" before earnest use at a short strip. He'd seen others dance power and brakes, taxiing with tail in the air. He knew that too much brake would push the prop into the ground, not enough and the tail rolled boringly on the ground. He also knew that too much power pushed the plane too fast and not enough left the plane sitting there. After trial waving up and down he found the sweet spot and taxied, tail high to the far end of the 3,000-foot runway. The professional felt good mastering the esoteric heights of his trade. He turned and finessed the throttle and pedals to return on just the two main wheels.

So, this is what it felt like to graduate to the big leagues. He smiled, removed his helmet, and waved to a colleague who probably witnessed this right-of-passage. But no smile crossed the man outside. Instead, with set jaw and wide eye he grabbed a fire extinguisher, ran to the plane, and sprayed the landing gear. The pilot jumped out to see white mist smoother the last flames.

Professional aviators know that knowledge is, indeed, power and safety. Unfortunately, its pride can obscure the truth that knowledge is always partial. We don't know what we don't know. Knowledge submitted to Christ's love, on the other hand, humbles us and opens a channel of intimacy with God that is not available any other way.

So, what happened the last time you discovered that you didn't know what you didn't know?

Proverbs 22:29   Galatians 6:1-5   Romans 10:1-4
2 Timothy 2:15   2 Corinthians 10:1-6

21. Hiding Places

Hiding places abound. Samuel anointed Saul as king of Israel. God gave him free reign saying, "Once these signs are fulfilled, do whatever your hand finds to do, for God is with you." Saul clearly saw God's certain ability and purpose. Did Saul hiding among coronation-day's baggage reveal humility or unbelief? Neither. God gave Saul victories, but also granted the deepest desire of his heart—his own way.

Rahab hid three times. She covered the spies, and then concealed family while her Jericho life fell around her. She, too, saw God's plan, when she confessed to her guests, "The Lord your God is God." Then, He gave her freedom to expose her heart. She rejected her experience with fierce, lusty warriors and the solid, unassailable might of their stone walls. Instead, she chose to hide in the promise of a God she'd never seen.

Dream-roots anchor in the soul's depth. When they collide with reality and die or, even scarier, succeed, what hiding place conceals us? We can manufacture an attainable call under the politically acceptable guise of meekness. But whose soul is it anyway? If it's ours, go ahead, hide in the manageable, keeping image intact, preserving name and throne. He, in turn, grants our wish and hides from us until we have our fill. However, if we surrender to Him, only one course remains open. Kick off the jar. Expose the light and hang on for a wild, dangerous ride. When embarrassment, failure, and death threaten, He entreats us to hide with Him and run into the shadow of His wings.

So, what chasm do you dangle over?

**Joshua 2:1-21   Luke 6:26   Judges 7:15-19   Luke 8:16
1 Samuel 10:20-22   1 Corinthians 6:19-20   Psalm 32:7
Galatians 2:20   Proverbs 16:25**

22. You Can't Get Lost

Life seems simple when you fly. Takeoff, turn to 135 degrees and climb to 5,500 feet. After thirty minutes Copataza slides under the left wing. Turn right, follow the river, and in another five minutes, pass over Mashient. Gently lower the nose until the vertical speed indicator settles on a 500-foot per minute descent, and clock nine minutes more. Voilá, Charapacocha appears magically out of the jungle with the plane at pattern altitude. A clear lesson emerges. Fly straight enough to hold heading, climb high enough to miss hard things, keep track of the time, and you will reach your destination. You can't get lost.

The Christian life, at first, appears the same—follow Jesus, and you will get to Heaven. You can't get lost. Guaranteed. But then it gets complicated. God's will doesn't eliminate ours, it becomes one more choice. We quickly learn that His way works and ours doesn't. So, naturally, we spend lots of time asking, seeking, and knocking. And a happy day dawns when we discern what He wants. But during the party the old man sneaks up unnoticed and says, "Thanks, Lord! I'll get right on this." Then, he picks up the ball and runs like crazy.

Eagerness to reach the goal tricks us into trying to accomplish it ourselves. But remembering that we can accomplish exactly nothing apart from Him renews our perspective.

So, what are you waiting on Him to do through you?

**Joshua 24:15   Colossians 3:5-11   John 15:1-8   James 4:4
Romans 6:5-7**

22

23. The Right Tool

Right tools bring joy, but wrong tools fail. Dust china cabinets with feathers, not brooms. Pound nails with hammers, not screwdrivers. Wash dishes with sponges, not grinders. Eliminate flies with swatters, not shotguns. God's kit includes every tool we need for life. So, for example, we manipulate creation with strength, not wishing. Twist a lid, open a jar. Burn gasoline, fly a plane. Keep running, complete a race. Work hard, make money. Out maneuver the competition, win a lover. If we change things by strength, can we change more things with more strength? Christ our Lord is strong, but so is our enemy, Satan. If the stronger devil beats us, does Christ beat him by even greater strength? Even God says, "Go in the strength of the Lord."

But what is the strength of the Lord? More muscle? Greater force of personality? Psychic power? Greater endurance? God designed strength—as we understand it—for use exclusively within creation, not without. When we call it our ultimate tool, we shut heaven's door and limit ourselves to a fight within the ropes of Satan's smack-down ring. Fortunately, two different, less appealing, tools in the kit do open the door—weakness and waiting.

Surrender strength and watch weakness attract His authority. He speaks of things that are not as though they were and creates something out of nothing. He says neither might nor power prevail, only His Spirit. Then, wait for Him, no one else. He gives new strength, eagle-wing strength, just the tool we need for mortality's journey.

So, now that you abandoned your chariots, chased off your horses, and stand exposed on the battlefield, how do you see Him prevailing against the advancing horde?

Psalm 20:7   Romans 4:17   Isaiah 40:27-31
1 Corinthians 1:26-31   Zechariah 4:6

24. Pointed Illusion

The pilot pushed the Saberliner throttles forward and relaxed only a little. The Army's Commanding General stayed too long. Now he, the aerial chauffeur, had to turn this jet into a time machine. *Okay, what can I do?* he asked himself. *Let's see ... skip the fuel stop; there's enough. Forget the airways; fly direct.* They could still make the meeting if everything went right. Later, still making it and only twenty-three miles from the capital city, he called approach control with his deepest, in-complete-charge voice. Earlier, the enroute controller had mentioned something about weather. But he didn't need any holding delays. And, he realized, he didn't have enough fuel for a missed approach or flight to an alternate field. This one had to count.

"The airport is below minimums. What are your intentions?" the local controller asked.

"Canceling instrument flight plan. I'll complete the approach visually," he answered. Forward pressure with his left hand eased the nose over as he descended fast, feeling for the ceiling below. He broke into murky haze 1,000 feet below the glide slope, searching for the familiar shape of mountain ridge on the left with the open space to the right. *Where is it?* he muttered to himself, wet beads popping out of brow and palm. Suddenly a dim, darker gray silhouette appeared on the right. *Right?* he asked himself. *No time, turn now. Looks ok, but ...* "The runway's there," he said confidently to the co-pilot as he pointed the nose where the runway would appear.

"Gear down, complete final landing check," he commanded. He scanned the panel once more, and then looked up in time to see the surprised face as he entered the apartment window.

When we beat reality into the shape we desire, we create only enticing illusions. Fortunately, if we choose to listen, the Holy Spirit stays our fervent hammering and points us back to The Truth.

So, how's He pointing you these days?

**2 Chronicles 35:20-23   Proverbs 21:5   Proverbs 14:12
Romans 1:24-25   Proverbs 15:22   James 1:22-25**

25. Glory Hogs

"There's no manna!" Tira burst into the tent, breathless.

"What do you mean, there's no manna?" she asked, annoyed, without looking up. This girl would tell her the sun was missing if she could get out of work.

"I looked everywhere. We all did. It's just not there. What are we going to eat?"

Her daughter's trembled question sunk doubt's claw into her own heart. What's wrong? They walked across the river, and no one got wet. As soon as they were out of the channel, back came the water, high and furious. Then, all the men   . what a bloody, messy affair. At least they'd quit moaning and were walking again. They ate the Passover the day before yesterday. Surely that would satisfy Him. What now? She sighed, turned towards Tira, shook her head slightly, and then looked down again at the roasted grain. Wonderful stuff. It was so good to taste something new, different. But was God mad? Weren't they supposed to eat it? The Levites said it was okay … What was going on?

"Trust Me!" the Lord commands. "Rest in Me." "Lay down your burden." "Watch my salvation." "Cast your cares on me." Manna fits those thoughts. If the Lord provided manna, why did He stop? Why doesn't He provide it now? Why did He say we can eat only by the sweat of our brow? Is He making some kind of joke when He says our hunger drives us on? What do we have to do to eat? Rest or work?

Wrong question. The goal is not to get the goods. The goal is trust. When we walk the barren waste with 6 million mouths to feed, He rains down what we need. But delivering manna everyday did not build trust. Neither does hard work. Instead, He designed life carefully to always contain a choice. The fruit comes from our cleverness, or His provision? Pick one. Ought to be easy, but we're glory hogs. Fortunately, He also crafted life to keep us just a bit off balance. We hunger for a peace that comes only after crawling off our throne—again—and giving it back to Him—again.

So, how's He equipping you today?

Joshua 5:2-12   Philippians 3:17-21   Psalm 127:1-2
2 Thessalonians 3:6-10   Matthew 11:25-28   1 Peter 5:7

26. Graceful Attitude

We pilots train to recognize and control three aspects of 'attitude flying:' nose position above, on, or below the horizon; wing bank left, center, or right of vertical; and the amount of power between idle and full. We quickly learn that even small attitude variations produce large performance changes. Exceed the specified pitch angle for a maximum-angle climb and the airplane stalls and falls. Exceed the critical bank angle in a tight, level turn and pull the wings off. Discerning the difference between a maximum performance attitude and disaster demands hours of practice.

As successful missionary candidates, we demonstrate attitudes with focus, determination, and diligence. We consistently control our time, finances, knowledge, skill, and natural impulses. But only a few degrees separate this maximum performance configuration from calamity. The counterfeit distorts the correct attitude ever so slightly. Our old nature embraces the lie, then religion rewards us. The subtle forgery adds the thought, "God owes me something for services rendered. I deserve His favor because I've been good. I should be blessed because I've followed the rules."

We hide in rules because grace doesn't seem fair. Our reborn spirit, on the other hand, confesses our weakness, sinfulness, and total dependence.

So, how do you see His grace adjusting your attitude?

Exodus 2:11-15   Galatians 3:1-5   Matthew 24:4-8   1 John 2:26-27 Luke 11:42

27. Remodel or Die

Remodeling takes work. Pull up flooring. Pry off molding. Remove cabinets. Cut through wall sheet-rock. Curl hands around the exposed edge and pull hard. Large chunks fall with a satisfying crash and lots of dusty pieces. The walls' bones lie bare and exposed. Remove the wires and stub off plumbing. The quick, fun, brute-force method uses the inelegant, but effective sledgehammer. Swing hard. Knock the studs free; remove the nails later. Run wires for new lights and fill gaps in the ceiling. Then tape, texture, and repaint. Install new flooring and cabinets. Clean up the mess, and, behold, an open, fresher, much nicer room. Your sweaty effort earned a place of rest and beauty for friends and family.

The Christian walk seems much the same way. New life possibilities open in bright contrast to the putrid cesspool we leave behind. Then, the realization of the behavior He expects sinks in. Love your neighbor. Turn the other cheek. Give to him who asks. Live faithfully. Treat others kindly. He even says that a wise man keeps himself under control.

Not easy, but we can do self-control. Throw out all the old stuff. Take out a wall. Add a window. New cabinets look nice and the lights really brighten up the place. Looks good, even classy. Except that the lights flicker a lot. No problem. Invite guests only in daylight. And the cabinet sags at one end. No problem. Tap a shim under the foot. But that sinks down into rotten flooring instead. Hide it with a plant?

Repairing repaired repairs never ends, and we eventually admit that the most carefully applied whitewash flakes when painted over slime. In fact, remodeling our old nature never succeeds.

The goal is not to renew, rejuvenate, or restore. Instead, He says, "Count yourselves dead and allow Me to live within you." He replaces rotten wood with a living tree fed by life's clear river, producing wondrous fruit that shines no matter how dark the night.

So, despite your best efforts, what strangely marvelous orb grows at the end of your new branches?

Matthew 7:15-20   Romans 6:5-11   Matthew 23:27-28
Galatians 2:20   John 15:1-8   Revelation 22:1-6

28. Course Correction

The pilot stared hard at ambiguous gray overhead. Systems like this one—from the south—often meant two to four weeks of rain and caught-up maintenance. Their route lay to the south, towards deteriorating weather. Could he get this missionary there before the jungle closed down? Then, inspiration. Instead of flying the regular dogleg route south to Huasaga and then a hard left for the quick descent into Surikenza, he could go direct. Finding it shouldn't be that hard, just hold heading like a Pharisee and keep track of time.

In the air, a dark, sullen wedge of glowering clouds forced him lower. No rain yet and visibility was okay. Gentle pressures on the rudder pedals kept it straight. Finally, time's up. Look for the strip. Nothing left, nothing ahead, bank right and … nothing right. Okay, the wind must be strong. Keep flying straight, keep looking. One minute, nothing. Two minutes, nothing. Three … Four? Something's not right. Okay, going direct was a bad idea, so let's turn right for Huasaga. Can't miss anything that big. One minute, two, three, no Huasaga … Not good. The view to the south looked worse. No time to return to the starting point. Then he saw a strip—neither his destination nor his turning point. In fact, he didn't recognize it at all, nor could he find a likely candidate on his chart.

He stuffed Captain's pride into his flight bag and landed. Indians ran to the plane. The missionary asked, in their language, if they could tell him the name of their fine airstrip. Stunned blank stares, pass the information, more silence, and then the guffawing laughter that looks the same in any language. There, on the chart, he located it. Still way north because of the wind, he flew five more minutes south to Huasaga. Then, turn left to 103 degrees, count off three minutes and Surikenza appeared. At this low altitude, the narrow opening in the trees was only visible from this angle, no other.

Sometimes, despite deepest desire and strongest intent we can't get there from here. God's path leads us to a place He knows we can find. Then, He gives us a course adjustment so we approach His destination from an angle that makes it visible to us. If we went direct, we wouldn't recognize it even if we stumbled across it.

So, when goals turned into waypoints, what new goals materialized after you were obedient to make the turn?

Genesis 37:1-37; 39:1-45:28   Acts 16:6-10   Acts 9:1-19

29. Word Portals

Sometimes, we think of heaven as a better version of here. And we regard Jesus as ourselves, only kinder, stronger, and generally better. We speak glibly, claiming that our sight of mystery's visible edge equals understanding. Actually, the revelation He permits nearly drowns us. More would destroy us. He warned Moses, "You cannot see my face, for no one may see me and live." How then can He promise that the pure in heart will see Him? After death? Sure. But what about exhortations to seek His face now? Sounds like telling kids to play with matches in the fuel shed.

Fortunately, He provides a way where none exists. Each instance of God's Word in our world joins us to His realm—a reality so different that our universe barely contains the idea. Open Word portals become conduits spewing out geysers of His nature and Kingdom, lighting up darkness and comforting broken hearts. He, Himself, is that Word convicting and cleansing, edifying and healing. His Word lives, feeding the dead with life until they breathe again. Through it, He brings hope, joy, peace and opens blind eyes. Even the deaf hear Him.

He calls us doorkeepers and entrusts us with keys. Reading turns locks, doing pulls doors open. The gushing flood transforms us until He returns. Then we shall be like Him and see Him as He is.

So, what hatches have you opened in your ship of life lately?

**Exodus 33:20   Matthew 4:4   Psalm 27:8-9   Matthew 5:8
Isaiah 43:18-19   Ephesians 5:25-27   John 1:1-2   1 John 3:2**

30. Safety Numbs

Longing fingers, sore from clutching airport fence, at last became trembling hands gripping first solo flight controls. New ability didn't just demonstrate new knowledge. It marked the birth of a sky-creature—sibling of the wind—at home with the clouds. Then, too many days plodded between flights while too few moments raced between propeller's first and last turns. Continually freshened, joy revealed deeper meaning. Like new love's desire, flying threatened to fulfill and consume everything at once. The one certainty became that there could never be enough, let alone too much.

Years later and half a planet away, another landing at a mud hole, running ahead of advancing rain. Touch brakes, slide a bit sideways, release, and then push in earnest, spraying wet, muddy grass. Shut down and hop to the ground. Let's see, who gets out here? One knee in mud, pull cargo from pod. The passenger says it's not his. Second knee in mud, head and both arms way in, pull out his stuff. Glance again at darker sky, replace first boxes. Room for only one more person, but two want to go. Wait while they decide under lowering clouds. Finally, load new cargo, new passenger, slosh to takeoff position and push the throttle forward. Then, do it again—many times. Is this the fifth or eleventh landing today? Only the flight sheet knows for sure. After 2,000 hours, 10,000 landings, and a body tired from too many adrenaline rushes, joy becomes just a job.

We, the privileged of creation, live in the Lord's family secure from prowling lions. But that safety numbs us when we forget our rescue. Some, who still live apart from the Lord, thirst for righteousness more desperately than the saints. Our world culture says that we should never have to want, so lost hunger becomes normal. We mistake dullness for peace and gain courage to flirt with unrighteousness.

But when you recall the joy of becoming a new heaven-creature what does your longing for justice and His right ways show you?

**Matthew 8:5-13   Romans 8:37-39   Acts 17:31
Revelation 2:1-7**

31. Successful Lies

He shook a finger straight at the pocked face across from him and said, "Look at you, the big man! You're bankrupt. You lost your family. You're covered with scabby pus. You're a mess! And why? Everyone knows that God works according to one simple rule—do right things, receive good; do wrong things, receive bad. Yet you keep moaning that it's not fair. Give it up, already! It's plain to everyone but you. If you mess up, you pay the price." He paused, overwhelmed again by his friend's grief. "Look," he said softly, "confess whatever it is you did and God will forgive you. You don't have to stay like this, Job."

A few hundred years later, weary travelers staggered into the center of camp, surrounded by guards. "Where you boys from?" the leader asked them.

"A long way from here," they said with exhausted resignation.

"Oh, yeah, how do we know that?" the leader quizzed.

They tiny band looked at each other with disbelief. "Well, ah, look at our stuff. It's all worn out. Our coats are thin, and our shoes full of holes. They were new when we started this trip."

Another added, "Here, look at what's left of our food. It's moldy now but was fresh when we left."

Then the elder traveler spoke up, "We're not trying to cause trouble, sir. But we've spent a long time getting here just so we could talk to you. We're from a place far away you've probably never heard of. It's called Gibeon."

Joshua scratched his beard, thought for moment, and then said, "Ok, the guard here will see that you get some water and food. We'll talk some more when you've rested a bit."

Job's friends spoke correctly about God punishing sin. And Joshua and his advisors also correctly understood that bread needs time to mold and shoes need miles to wear through. They looked for and reached logical conclusions from indisputable facts. Unfortunately, they forgot that distorted truth supports successful lies. Real truth, on the other hand, comes not by looking at facts alone, but by touching the Truth Himself.

So, what mirages has God's character dispelled around you lately?

Joshua 9:3-27   John 1:3-5; 9:39; 12:25; 14:6-7; 16:33   Job 11:1-20

32. Constant Practice

Two pursuits require constant practice, three never rest: Flying airplanes in the bush, playing musical instruments for an audience, and walking with God.

Remembering that final airspeed varies between 55 and 60 knots, depending upon gross aircraft weight, is not the same thing as recognizing the edge of 'the settle' while playing the throttle on a bumpy approach. Reaction trails need and wheels touch only in the general vicinity of the target spot. Amateur hides professional.

Remembering Beethoven's "Fur Elise" is not the same thing as producing the smooth parade of notes up and down the keyboard. Nervous fingers hesitate, forgetting their path. They arrive only more or less on time. Parody eclipses masterpiece.

Remembering God's direction when He led us to our ministry is not the same thing as having His Word now, in the heat. No wisdom comes forth; no insight enlightens. We give all we have—sympathy and a shrug. Emptiness covers filling.

None of these remain current by themselves. They offer us only two choices—push and grow, or loaf and slide. Fortunately, He calls and equips us to climb.

So, what do you see when you look up?

1 Corinthians 3:1-3   2 Timothy 2:25; 3:1-17; 4:1-5
Ephesians 2:8-10   Hebrews 4:14-16; 13:20-21

33. Cause and Effect

We know the secret to success: pick up good pieces, assemble correctly, and point in the desired direction. Every action results in something. Choose the right effort; reap a good reward. Archimedes taught us that, given a big enough lever and a place to stand, we could even move the Earth. The proper combination of cause and effect works for everything—Legos®, houses, quilts, money, and life. But secret knowledge addicts us to success. We demand it as our right and then rage at God's injustice when we fail. We manipulate universal building blocks but forget that batteries do not power creation while God sits back watching it scoot about heaven's floor.

Instead, God invests Himself into His creation. He holds everything together, sustains all things, and fills everything in all ways. He holds protons and neutrons together with the strong nuclear force. Atoms interact chemically because He exerts the electromagnetic force, and His gravity keeps the Earth within a narrow, life-permitting orbit. Neurons fire, eyes see, ears hear, and hearts beat.

If the Divine hand that glues galaxies together also sustains us, why do we fear that money, strength, and life's purpose depend upon our sweaty smarts? Has the sun ever risen late? The simple truth is "Unless the LORD builds the house, its builders labor in vain. Unless the LORD watches over the city, the watchmen stand guard in vain. In vain you rise early and stay up late, toiling for food to eat—for he grants sleep to those he loves."

So, when was the last time His hope surprised you, close at hand, vanquishing your despair?

**Psalm 127:1-2   John 3:16   Proverbs 10:4; 13:4; 19:3; 20:4
Colossians 1:15-17   Matthew 6:25-34**

34. Hard Places

We live within creation's cage: the double twins of space and time, matter and energy. Their impartial rule treats us all alike. Money, hours, and strength go only until spent. Do the taxes, wash clothes, or hold your honey? Choose one. You can take enough fuel to go the distance, but what cargo stays behind? You can make the extra landing for the patient, but sunset will stop the flight short of the hospital. Limits dog life. Neither desire nor worthy need gains their attention. Their hard places define humanness and teach the brutal lesson quickly: There is not enough to go around. Get yours while you can.

God, on the other hand, lavishes. He pours Himself out, shamelessly ignoring conservation, moderation, and budgets. If limits define neither His character nor His nature, how do we reconcile the humanness we're trapped in with His call to live in the Spirit now?

He calls it stewardship—constraining ourselves to mortality's limits in order to minister eternity. He didn't call us to hide our talents in holes, fearful that they might run out or evaporate. Instead, He tells us to administer His grace that feeds thousands from a kid's small lunch with such wild exuberance, celebration, and abandon that even the dead wake up.

So, what's it like swimming in the torrent of His blessing?

Matthew 6:1-4; 25:14-30   Ephesians 1:3
Luke 6:37-38; 14:25-33   1 Peter 4:10-11   John 6:5-13

35. Captured by Good

Sometimes good captures us—the partner mission's success; a neighbor's new car and paid off mortgage; a coworker's great health, a clean house and well behaved kids; a wide-screen, high-definition, surround-sound home theater system. God gives good things, but the fight begins when the cute singer on the worship team expels the song from imagination's space. Wrestle the thought and smash temptation to the floor. Don't look there, turn the other way. But the other way is not like the other cheek. The beautiful monster escapes the restraining grasp and dances before our hearts with easy insolence—again and again and again.

Denying a good thing's existence contradicts the truth. But the truth that God wired us to recognize the good He created sets us free. We discovered helium on the Sun before we found it on Earth—not because it wasn't here, but because we didn't know how to see it. Likewise, we overcome distraction by learning to see the best, located beyond the good, just like the crew of C.S. Lewis' ship, *Dawn Treader*, saw Aslan's land beyond and higher than the sun. On the other side of good, we find His best containing all good things for enjoyment in their proper place, at their proper time. Out of context, good things bedevil, ensnare, and distract. Submitted to Him, however, they bless.

So, how is Jesus appearing beyond, over, and through the unruly mob before you?

**Leviticus 26:4-5   Luke 14:26   Psalm 23   Romans 8:28   Isaiah 30
1 Tim 4:4   Matthew 6:25-27; 7:9-11   Hebrews 9:11-14; 16:25-27**

36. Point of View

In the air, pilots survey vast panoramas, confident of encompassing perspective. But they miss the approaching storm, invisible behind the overcast. Mothers, out foxed by precocious toddlers, believe life consists of jelly smeared CDs and melted crayons smashed into wads of unmatched socks. They forget the world of humans taller than three feet, who speak in whole sentences. From the valley on the west, the snow-covered volcano Cotopaxi stands almost pastoral. Cultivated fields surround its base and climb its sides. From the high mesa on the east, however, it resembles a Mars probe photo. Same mountain; different points of view.

God does not have a point of view, nor even multiple points of view. He made points-of-view and set them within creation. Created reality, in turn, limits us to only one place at a time and only one time called "now." We behold all of life from one, single vantage point. Because we live under creation's constraint, we invite difficulty when we declare our point of view the sole correct among many. Worse, we cultivate disaster when we assume others see life from the same point we occupy.

Fortunately, He gave us a way to navigate through. Pilots radio what they see across the jungle, and everyone gets the big weather picture. Moms escape—thanks to smart dads—and assure each other that the rational, adult experience still exists. Believers share submitted lives, the Holy Spirit assembles the aggregate expression, and God's plan moves forward.

So, how's He moving through your team?

2 Kings 6:8-22   Romans 4:16-17   Isaiah 55:8-9
2 Corinthians 4:18   Jeremiah 33:2-3   Revelation 22:12

37. Who He Calls

God says, "Fear not, for I have redeemed you; I have summoned you by name; you are mine. When you pass through the waters, I will be with you; and when you pass through the rivers, they will not sweep over you. When you walk through the fire, you will not be burned; the flames will not set you ablaze." Sounds good, especially for encouraging others setting out on grand adventures and hopeless quests. But why does our response to His call often leave us feeling rolled, spindled, and mutilated? What happened to supplying all our needs? Or granting wisdom, comfort, or money enough to do what He told us to do?

The answer partially appears, of course, once we recognize the disparity between our desires, wearing a needy-cloak, and His knowledge. But after life works that lesson in us, we still wonder—secretly—at the difference. Seems like He continually keeps us off balance—demanding more than our ability and providing less than our need.

Truth's less obvious portion reveals itself in just who, exactly, He calls. Human eyes see destitute beggars and lost fools forming the bulk of God's Kingdom. God, on the other hand, calls the redeemed to do the impossible: those bought for a price to pass through the fire, His saints to cross raging waters, His ambassadors to confront the kingdoms of darkness. Yes, He dragged us as miserable, wretched worms from Hell's cesspool. But then, He adopted us as sons, made us citizens of His Kingdom, and filled us with Himself, with His divinity, power, wisdom, knowledge, and truth. We feel off balance here because we no longer stand on Earth. Rather, He planted our feet on the Rock of Heaven's high places. We speak His words to those clinging to a sinking ship's tilted deck.

So, what happened the last time you realized that the ground was no longer your foundation?

Isaiah 43:1-2 2 Corinthians 5:16-21 Mark 6:6-13
Philippians 4:18-19 1 Corinthians 1:18-31 Hebrews 11:1-39

38. Invisible Matter

Dark matter and dark energy make up most of our universe, but elude detection, neither seen nor measured. Only their effect on surrounding galaxies betrays their presence. The morning breeze passes through open windows, invisible. Only billowing curtains and wet field smell translate its call of faraway adventure.

God's favor flows around us continually, soaking everything with His goodness yet, like a symphony to the deaf, passes unnoticed. Nor would any even suspect what they miss except for His distributors. He designed each of us to receive a specific piece of that blessing and then, in turn, dispense our unique portion. No two are identical, but together, we administer His grace in its various forms.

Persecution, resentment, discouragement, poor health, failure, and frustration with life make performing our primary job difficult. Good times can make it even harder, unless we remember the wonder of revealed light.

So, what kind of candle did Jesus give you to wave against the blackness?

Matthew 5:45; 13:22   Hebrews 2:1-4   Romans 11:28-32; 12:3-8 1 Peter 4:8-11

39. Wave Slap

"Are we getting anywhere?" Thomas groaned pulling an oar. "We've been rowing all night." The windy darkness hid Peter's wry smile as he pulled with the others not wasting energy on wit. Dawn couldn't be far off, and they weren't even halfway yet. He guessed three, maybe three and a half miles at best.

Suddenly, James let out a long, low moan, "Nooo …"

Oh, not again, Peter thought. Some people just never get used to boats. "Just do it over the side!" he growled.

But then, the others took up the chorus. "What is it?" one cried. "What? What? I still don't see anything?" another complained.

"There, right there!" James dropped his oar and jabbed emphatically with both arms while trying to stand against the tossing deck.

The boat pitched and tipped, losing all headway as the men leapt up crying "Demon!" and "Ghost!" Peter stopped rowing and, still seated, turned slowly. There, off the starboard side, movement in the shredded, cloudy moonlight. It looked like a man on a walk, about to pass them by. Something about the gait, though, the way the arms swung loosely like a child with nothing to hide, drew him. Could it be? Of course! It had to be!

"Lord, is that you?" Peter called out.

"Take courage. It is I. Don't be afraid," the wind whipped voice responded.

"Lord, if it really is you, then," he took a breath, "command me to come to you."

"Come," the man beckoned simply.

Certainty. Absolute, solid certainty banished question and quiz— the same that filled him on the beach that first day. A silent island in the chaos, he rose, swung a leg over the side, stood, and brought the other out to pace towards his desire. Neither hard nor soft, not squishy nor moving, but solid, the surface under his sandals held him more easily than rock or heath. As he crossed the distance, Jesus beamed a broad, delighted, open tooth, laughing grin. Peter wanted to run, skip, and dance all at once, but then another movement flashed in the corner of his eye.

He turned just as the wave slapped his face. Then he saw another, and the one behind it, and the next one after that. He knew the sea. He knew storms. He knew what they could do, what they did do. He could still see lost friends' bloated, half eaten, rotting bodies washed up with garbage at water's edge. His feet seemed mushy, stuck somehow. His knees were wet, now his waist. Panicked and sinking, he turned back to Jesus, crying, "Lord, save me!"

Jesus reached out and raised him back up. "You of little faith," he said. "Why did you doubt?" Together they walked back to the boat, but the Lord's smile lingered even as they climbed in.

We believe the rules of our realm, but Jesus demands we follow the laws of His. How can we do both? Should we try? Great faith is not blind faith. It does not say that heavenly principles negate creation's regulations; we are all under authority, and all authority comes from Him. Nor does it demand the impossible—the laws of physics are the same for everybody. Instead, it understands that Kingdom principles under-lie our world and set its limits. Trusting the One who tells us that 'anything is possible to him who believes' reveals the key. And trust, of course, depends entirely upon Whom we know.

So, when you're with Him, how far from the boat does He lead you?

Isaiah 55:1-13   John 1:1-5; 14:1-4   Matthew 10:2-4; 14:22-36; Romans 15:13; 17:20   Hebrews 1:1-3   Luke 7:1-10

40. Accustomed to Rescue

The Samaritan forgot when he'd chosen shuffle over stride. Pain hadn't stopped him. Dragging his drooping left foot across hot, sharp rocks produced no sensation at all. After a dozen falls gave as many painless, oozing wounds, sliding seemed safer. He clutched his robe close with the remainder of his left hand. His right hand—still with solid thumb and index finger—raised, swinging his staff forward in the familiar cadence—thump, slide; thump, slide. Sometimes he'd keep rhythm with one of his Hebrew companions— until they noticed. He thought it fun, but they said fun was not for punished sinners.

They topped the path's low rise and saw, heading towards the same village, a small, excited crowd. Why did all those faces gleam, he wondered? Malik answered, "Because they eat every day and oil their hair. Even you'd glitter." The others snickered.

No, something looked different. There, the one in front, the one the others looked to . Could it be? Sudden, hot hope burst out as he cried with more strength than he owned, "Jesus, Master, have pity on us!"

His companions joined the clamber, the crowd stopped, and the man called back to them, "Go, show yourselves to the priests." Kind direction compelled more fiercely than shouted command. As they wheeled about, he stepped high, with strong, unscarred foot. The Hebrews ran on laughing and leaping, but he stopped short, gawking at ten whole toes and ten straight fingers. Then, he turned again, ran down the hill and threw himself at the man's feet, weeping and laughing an unbroken string of thanks.

So, what happened the last time that you, a child of the King, realized you'd lost wonder and gratitude and had, instead, grown accustomed to salvation and used to redemption?

Genesis 40:12-23   Romans 1:21   Ecclesiastes 9:13-16
John 14:5-14   Luke 12:19; 17:11-19; 24:25

41. Bleating of Sheep

Saul's long legs crossed the room in three strides. He turned, paced to the opposite wall and returned again. "You're sure it's him?" he asked the soldier standing before him.

The guard frowned at the tense reception. "Ah, yes, sir. Abijah spotted him on the trail from Carmel. He has good eyes and knows Samuel's walk." More carefully, he added, "We thought you'd want to know right away, sir. He'll be here soon ..."

"Yes, yes, of course." Saul dismissed him with a distracted wave, stared at nothing, and chewed a fingernail. Outside, shepherds organized flocks and herds under careful, appraising eyes. The best would be sacrificed, of course, but the very good remainder ... Well, the men expected their right of plunder to be honored. Besides, taking care of Israel's defenders made good sense for both morale and the economy. It was the wise and prudent thing to do. Samuel would understand good stewardship. Sandals slapped through the door.

"The Lord bless you!" he beamed to the visitor. "I have carried out the Lord's instructions."

But Samuel asked, "What then is this bleating of sheep in my ears? What is this lowing of cattle that I hear?"

We know the story, but the question comes up: If God called His anointed king's stewardship rebellion instead, what chance do we have to tell the difference?

We, enlightened, powerful, and wise, rarely worry for food and usually hold pestilence at bay. We select a job from many options and choose the mate who sparkles our eye. Start a business. Buy a car. Move to another city. Take a year off to find ourselves. Try a lo-carb diet. Get an education to learn the secrets of the universe. We know why it rains, why grass grows, why bumblebees fly and stars shine. Matter, time, and energy bend ever more sharply to our will. Each mystery we conquer abolishes yet another of God's hiding spaces, relegating Him to life's remaining unknowns. Our mastery of life's smorgasbord grows with each retreat of understanding's limits until, finally, we believe that we actually do dominate it.

But despite our steady victory over ignorance, fear, and want, Jesus continues to counsel us that "apart from him we can do nothing." He makes it clear that dependence trumps knowledge and obedience surpasses even good stewardship.

So, what's He done lately to reminded you of Who's really in control?

**1 Samuel 15:1-35   1 Corinthians 8:1-3; 13:2   John 15:5
Ephesians 3:14-19**

42. Good Will

Mathias sat at last, squeezing among huddled shepherds, circling the tiny fire.

"Dog?" his brother asked without looking up.

"Two," he replied, pulling cloak against the wind.

Mathias let out a long breath, relaxing only to watchful dozing—his duty tonight. Eyes closed, he was ready.

Light flared! The fire? He stood up faster than eyes could open. A man, tall and gleaming, loomed before them, terrible, yet with hand raised, palm out. "Do not be afraid," he assured them. "Behold, I bring you good news of great joy which will be for all the people; for today in the city of David there has been born for you a Savior, who is Christ the Lord."

Joy? What sort of gift, exactly, did the angel bring to "all the people"? Many see trouble; others live alone, in bitter deprivation. Those with time and means pursue happiness, but even the redeemed often fail to catch it. Did God make a cruel joke so He could laugh while we chase smoke?

Hardly. Joy comes neither by hunting a thing, nor by seeking a feeling. Pretending happiness during bad times creates only secret resentment that blessings and benefits rarely remedy. Joy, on the other hand, is the person Jesus—His real presence within us. That communion alone yields strength, fruit, and peace. Which, of course, demonstrates God's goodwill to all men.

So, what happened the last time you were drenched while drawing the waters of salvation?

**Luke 2:8-20   Acts 2:22-28   John 15:9-17; 16:19-24
Romans 5:1-8**

43. Newtonian Bias

Three things escape understanding, four remain a mystery: Particles that arrive before they leave, God's patience claimed as permission, Temptation called His leading, and a cold heart described as His peace.

We know that the cause happens first, followed by the effect. But quantum mechanics exposes our Newtonian-bias and details an absurd universe rebelling against common sense.

Likewise, at the beginning, we agreed to see things the Lord's way. But walking by His Spirit defies common sense. Our world-bias paints us at the center of creation and disposes us to favor counterfeits above reality. Distorted truth—far more dangerous than the obvious, outright lies we preach against—misplaces our confidence. We renege, ever so slightly, on total surrender and imagine successful negotiations for a few, small, reasonable terms. That blinds us to the trouble of divided loyalties. Choosing between Jesus and the Devil is easy. The hard fight lies in the subtle, half-conscious middle ground of mixed motivation. Locked heart chambers hide idols of significance, security, jealousy, and fear allowing them only to be fed regularly, but never brought to trial.

Fortunately, He said through James, "If any of you lacks wisdom, he should ask God, who gives generously to all without finding fault, and it will be given to him. But when he asks, he must believe and not doubt, because he who doubts is like a wave of the sea, blown and tossed by the wind. That man should not think he will receive anything from the Lord; he is a double-minded man, unstable in all he does."

So, how has He clarified your vision lately?

**Proverbs 14:12   1 Corinthians 4:1-5   Romans 2:1-4
1 Timothy 4:1-5**

44. Stellar Dust

Our solar system contains a lot of junk. Planets, moons, comets, and asteroids sail along in a pool, dirty with bits left over from creation and debris from celestial collisions. Engineers design space ships to withstand the constant cosmic sandstorm—less dense than the earthly variety, but much faster. Typical particles zip along at 20,000 miles per hour.

Fortunately, micrometeorites are tiny—one-quarter of a hair's thickness. But even little things can add up big. Every year, 30,000 tons (that's 16,700 gross weight Cessna 206's or 7 million gallons of milk) of extraterrestrial dust settles gently on oceans, fields, and rooftops.

God used some of that dirt when He formed "… the man from the dust of the ground and then breathed into his nostrils the breath of life …" His pouring divine spirit into stellar dust uniquely equipped us to manage His creation. He named us His world's rangers, His property's caretakers, and His vineyard's stewards. Our instructions? Administer, don't exploit; guide, don't abuse; shepherd, don't devour; wait for my return.

So, what happened the last time creation's groan stirred your quest for sonship?

Genesis 1:24-31; 2:4-25   Romans 8:18-27
Matthew 13:31-43; 25:34-40

45. Good Enough?

Our pastor asked us, "How good is good enough?" Good enough for what? Pleasing people? Earning a good-person reputation? Showing genuine kindness? All worthy, reachable goals. While pleasing people is one thing, getting into heaven is an entirely different matter. Standards, after all, restrict entrance. Fortunately, Jesus illuminates the bar clearly. He says, "Be perfect, therefore, as your heavenly Father is perfect." Unfortunately, while acting good pleases God, good acting doesn't get us to God. Jesus confirmed that no one acts or thinks good enough to make the cut. "Why do you call me good? No one is good—except God alone."

We know the Good News, of course. Forgiveness lifts us easily over the bar. Anyone can meet the requirements. No cost. No pedigree. Neither hoops nor exams. He lavishes His most precious gift on anybody who asks. And that gives us the key to transformation rather than phony disguise—the one way others might call us "little Christs." He uses us to pour out His ridiculously inappropriate forgiveness, drenching unsuspecting souls who commit unpardonable offenses with totally undeserved favor.

So, when was the last time someone ambushed you with His un-earnable grace?

Matthew 5:48   Acts 11:19-26   Mark 10:17-21
Romans 3:21-26; 5:12-21

46. Attack the Hill

The ski instructor commands, "Attack the hill!" Easy to say, standing on the flats. Harder to apply while hurtling down a snowy precipice, dodging trees and rocks. Yet, the truth is that putting weight on ski fronts gives control, leaning back throws it away. Stretching our face closer to up-rushing destruction offers safety, leaning back steals all chances. Leaning forward yields survival's only hope, leaning back bears only bad fruit.

Not exactly intuitive. Just like walking with God. He draws us surely, inexorably to Himself. We race through time towards a final meeting that seems so like destruction we name it death. Our self-instinct pulls us back, clawing at powdered snow on ice. Yet, seeing our plight, He calls out, "Lean forward!"

Madness? Hardly. Pressing faces forward, closer to Him, gives us control through life's treacherous curves. After all, He's the one who promised that if we lose our lives for His sake, we'll gain it.

So, the last time you found yourself flat on your back, speeding out of control, how did you find the courage to get up and lean forward?

Proverbs 16:25   John 5:16-30; 6:35-69; 8:50
Matthew 10:37-39   1 Corinthians 1:18-31

47. The Guards Slept On

Peter snapped awake, still feeling the blow. Light everywhere, brighter than day, but the guards slept on.

"Quick, get up!" the shining man commanded.

He turned, unrolling from chains to the one stand-able position. Wrists floated free as manacles clattered to the stone floor. Guards, swords at hand, still slept. No calls, no questions, no threats through the gate. Only brilliantly flooded silence.

"Get dressed. Follow me," the—angel maybe?—ordered.

Follow where? The other side of the cell? But his feet slid obediently across cold, slimy rock into sandals, and he pulled the cloak closer. They walked to the first gate, pushed it open and passed the guards. Nothing. On through the next gate without a word. Finally, the main prison gate to the city swung open without hands, still no out-cry raised an alarm, no challenge overtook them, no spear in back, no fist to face. They walked through the prison in blazing, silent light. A remarkable dream, he marveled. Wonder what it means? Something about freedom in the Spirit, surely. This feels so real. Definitely won't be fun waking up between those two soldiers again. His guide smiled as if hearing the thought then vanished leaving him alone in the dark street.

The truth is that we usually find only what we expect to see. When we go to Jesus, what do we expect? A political king, as the Israelites did? An early bridegroom, as the five foolish virgins did? A slain teacher as the disciples did? If we seek what Jesus can do for us, we'll find that all things, all ideas, all situations eventually fail. On the other hand, if we seek Jesus himself as our reward, expecting to find Him, He guarantees success—and throws in all the other stuff, too.

So, how has He surprised you with Himself lately?

Matthew 6:25-34; 25:1-13   Acts 12:1-11   John 10:1-18; 14:6-7

48. Searching for the Sun

He couldn't remember how long since the batteries quit and the long night engulfed him. Blackness, thick and absolute, hid everything. He pushed through tangled thorns, testing for holes. His fingers still encircled the useless, invisible flashlight. Fingers? Once more he wiggled them just beyond his nose. He saw nothing to confirm what only feeling and hope told him were there.

Suddenly, a branch snapped on his left. He tried to crouch, but massed branches pushed him back. Then, not caring what the night beasts heard, he cried between clenched teeth, "Lord, why didn't you make these batteries last? Why won't you make them work again? I need light!" More snaps, then unmistakable, measured steps closing in.

"Hey, mister," the little voice asked, "whatcha doing here?"

"Who are you?" he hissed. "And how can you see me?"

Giggling, she said, "Open your eyes, silly. You're in my mom's hedge."

Sometimes, when our way seems dark, we cry over dead batteries, ignoring the brilliant light already provided.

So, what happened the last time you found yourself searching for the sun with a candle?

**Proverbs 19:3   John 1:3-5   Matthew 13:36-43; 17:1-8
Revelation 1:12-16**

49. Solar Wind

Suddenly, Isaiah stood in the temple, now immense, filled with terrible, glorious light that pierced like a thousand caressing swords. Terrifying desire drew his eyes to the brilliant throne above the Ark. The Lord sat, splendid, more real than life, surrounded by the hosts of heaven. Isaiah's soul emptied in one agonized cry, "O' God! How can I see You and live?"

Indeed. The wise fear Him with good reason. Standing before life's Giver means also standing before life's Judge. No one hides. Everything opens. All pretense, lies, and sin evaporate, leaving only the holy. Yet, Isaiah lived. How?

The Sun beats our world with the fierce, one million mile-per-hour solar wind. The source of summer heat and meadow light also pummels us with radiation that sometimes fries satellites, disrupts radio systems, blackens cities, and damages major pipelines. It can destroy life as we know it. Yet, every plant and creature flourishes. How?

God formed this planet with a liquid iron core and a large moon to stir it. Their interaction creates a magnetic field surrounding the entire earth that points compass needles north, guides birds across continents, and, like a raincoat, deflects the solar wind. Likewise, Peter revealed God's survival gift, "All of you, clothe yourselves with humility toward one another, because, God opposes the proud but gives grace to the humble."

So, how has His mighty hand lifted you up lately?

Isaiah 6:1-8   1 Peter 1:3-9   Colossians 3:12-14   1 Peter 5:5-7

50. Unmasked Heart

In the hangar, he pulled the torque wrench, steadily increasing pressure until it clicked. "250 inch-pounds exactly," he said to himself, confirming both instrument and manual. But deep satisfaction evaporated as he remembered the evangelist's words, all too clear even in this newly acquired language. His stomach turned again, picturing going door-to-door with the congregation. "Lord," he implored, looking up, "why did you bring me here?"

Across town, his wife asked her neighbor over tea, "But I don't understand, yet. What finally gave you the courage to turn away from tradition and follow Jesus?"

The woman laughed, eyes twinkling above discreet, knowing smile, "You missionary couples treat each other so well. After a few years I knew it was your heart, not a mask. I wanted that."

We worry about ministry action, forgetting the Lord's promise to remain with us. And, in us. He goes where we go. He shines from hills we climb. His presence invades wilderness our feet tread. The truth is that the Lord's living water gushes from lives we live.

So, what happened the last time you tried to walk in someone else's gift?

Joshua 1:1-5   John 7:37-39; 13:34-35   Zechariah 14:3-9
Colossians 1:24-27   Matthew 5:14-16

51. Wind and Waves

At least he wasn't chained, not that it mattered much. Crashing water punctuated the wind's constant howl. The deck he lay on slid, jumped, fell, and rose again—sometimes with regular purposeful beat, other times mad and crazy. Paul wasn't sure how long since he'd eaten. Wonder if there's anything dry anywhere? Dry? There was an interesting thought. What was dry? Was there anywhere dry or was the entire universe just a malevolent, bucking gray sea twisted with angry gray sky? He thought he'd been on his way somewhere for some purpose, some really important purpose, but now ...

Suddenly, quiet, calm, warm brightness. Someone stood beside him. "Don't be afraid Paul. You must stand trial before Caesar; and God has graciously given you the lives of all who sail with you." He remembered where he was going, why, and, most importantly, Who sent him.

By itself, water lies flat. But, moving air pushes smooth ocean into troubled waves. Stronger wind racing over more miles of fetch for longer time grows bigger waves. Even light wind, given sufficient time and distance produces monstrous waves. The Southern Ocean completely circles the Earth below South America and north of Antarctica. No land mass impedes the eastward march of wind and water. Our planet's strongest winds and largest waves rampage unchecked around the circle of the world's fourth largest ocean.

Likewise, doubt's wind blows across our sea of thoughts. Unimpeded, lie's mounting waves circle our minds, hit from the right and slap from the left. Tossed up, dropped then pitched again, stinging spray confuses the familiar, batters confidence, feeds fear, and obscures even sun and stars. Where were we going? Was there anywhere else to go? Did anywhere else besides here even exist? Dark, crashing water smashes the compass, and we lose our course. Finally, a blow spins us sideways, a second tips us over, and the tempest swallows us.

Fortunately, the Lord gives many kinds of grace—goggles to see in pelting sea, stout compasses to guide in pitching craft, lights to shine in bedeviling dark, harbors to hide from violent storm, and—in the utmost extremity—breath for life in watery graves.

So, when was the last time you found yourself talking grace but living law?

Matthew 11:20-25   2 Corinthians 3:4-6   Acts 27:13-26

Ephesians 4:7-16   Romans 5:17   James 1:2-8

52. God Doesn't

God works on our behalf full-time, not just when:

Life flows badly; we fear the worst; the worst arrives; life flows well; we seek the best; the best arrives; we plead; we act right; we think right; we dream right; we pray; we sacrifice; we give; we love others; we love him; we follow him faithfully; we backslide; we repent; we try hard; we try harder.

God doesn't:

Get distracted; get overbooked; get confused; get tired; get tired of us; get too busy; get bored; forget us; forget to care; forget to act; forget the time; forget the context; forget the details; lose sight of us; lose us in the crowd; lose interest; have blind spots; have bad days; go on vacation; go somewhere else; go home; go away; go nuts; give up on us.

So, the last time you clawed desperately at precipice edge, how did you remember that His Kingdom has no cracks to fall through?

Matthew 28:16-20   Hebrews 13:4-8   John 10:27-30
1 Peter 3:12   Romans 8:31-39

53. The Nose Knows

Jacob watched his father eat. Even blind, he refused help, attacking the haunch with a grin unhidden by his gray beard. Wish he showed that kind of enthusiasm for me. Well, I'll show him. Someday he'll be proud of me, too. Besides, the blessing's mine. Esau didn't want it. So, I'm just collecting what's already mine.

"So, my son, come here, and kiss me so that I can bless you," Isaac said, suddenly setting the stripped bone aside.

Jacob's forehead popped wet beads. Lowering his voice to his brother's deeper timber, he replied "Yes, my father," as he shuffled forward in the ill-fitting suit. What was that furrow between the old man's sightless eyes? Did he suspect? Before he could evade, his father embraced him with surprising strength. Isaac said nothing, buried his face in the stolen tunic, and inhaled deeply. Heart pounding in ears, Jacob held his breath. Then slowly, his father relaxed the iron grip, sighed contentedly, and said, "Ah, the smell of my son …"

The olfactory nerve contains about ten million neurons that carry data from nose to brain. According to one theory, each neuron responds to only a single, specific shape of odor molecule, just as only one key opens any given lock. Most odor molecules twist in a complex mix of shapes that activate various combinations of neurons. Smell lasts more accurately in long-term memory than any other sense and touches emotions strongly. A sudden whiff triggers past feelings, making them intensely present. Cross-cultural smells delight or disgust us. Foreign body, street and market odors generate heart-deep judgments. Despite modern deodorant's drive to make us all equally nice, different odors still distinguish individual people and different cultures.

Likewise, God marks His people with distinctive scent. Paul wrote, "But thanks be to God, who always leads us in triumphal procession in Christ and through us spreads everywhere the fragrance of the knowledge of him. For we are to God the aroma of Christ among those who are being saved and those who are perishing. To the one we are the smell of death; to the other, the fragrance of life."

So, how does He make you and those around you an aromatic offering to Himself?

Genesis 27:1-29   2 Corinthians 2:14-17

54. A Monster

A monster lives in my closet; that one over there, behind the drape. I'd like to get rid of him, but he breathes fire, and his claws would rip me to shreds.

A monster lives in my closet. He roars, curses, and his smoke stinks. I'd like to get rid of him, but he's kind of big, and he might bite me.

A monster lives in my closet. He bangs on the door, scratches the paint, and, yesterday, dented the wall. I'd like to get rid of him, but I can't find the exterminator's number.

A monster lives in my closet. He makes rude noises, interrupts, and has lousy table manners. I'd like to get rid of him, but I don't know where to send him.

A monster lives in my closet. He whines in the most pitiful way. I'd like to get rid of him, but he'll track mud all over the carpet.

A monster lives in my closet. He's annoying and embarrassing. I'd like to get rid of him, but I'm busy today.

A monster lives in my closet, and if I don't feed him now, he'll pop out while company's here.

Monsters beat us when constrained. But eliminate closets and they fall, easy prey for God's grace.

So, what happened the last time you refused condemnation and ran, instead, to the cross that frees you from sin and death?

**Proverbs 28:13   Romans 8:1-4   Jeremiah 16:17
Colossians 1:15-20   Acts 19:17-20   I John 1:8-10**

55. Little Worm

Isaiah said, "Do not be afraid, O worm Jacob, O little Israel, for I myself will help you, declares the LORD, your Redeemer, the Holy One of Israel."

Great metaphor, Isaiah. It is nice to know that the Lord cares for us, and exaggeration does make a good illustration. But, 'worm? A little heavy on the condemnation, don't you think? We are, after all, created in His image. How about something we can identify with, something more like us?

Indeed. How about the common house dust mite (Dermatophagoides farinae)? This eight-legged creature inhabits carpets and bedding, consuming the three-tenths of an ounce of skin cells we shed everyday. The old ones live a month and grow to 16-thousandths of an inch long. That makes us 4,500 times bigger than the average mite. If they were six feet long, we'd be over five miles tall. Neither knowing nor caring, we feed them, yet they have no clue we exist. We're more like God than like mites.

Of course, they do demand food, air, water, and light and survive only in a narrow temperature range. And they inhabit the birth, life, and death cycle clearly, making them fellow prisoners with us in space-time. God, on the other hand, needs no food, no air, no water; He creates light, exists eternally, and defies measurement. The distance to the nearest edge of the home He made for us—think cardboard box with pencil-poked holes called 'The Observable Universe'—is 4,800,000,000,000,000,000,000,000,000 times bigger than we are. On that scale, we are indistinguishable from brother mite. Worm complements us.

Except for one small detail: He loves us.

He chooses us. He knows us. He reveals Himself to us. He takes us into His counsel. He calls us son, daughter, friend, and beloved. He permits, calls, even beseeches us to know Him. He seeks us out. He commands mercy and goodness to follow us all our days. He gave up His most precious possession to rescue us, His most ungrateful, rebellious, stiff-necked creatures.

Considering that, how is He, Himself, vanquishing fear to help you O little Israel?

**Isaiah 41:14   Romans 12:3   John 3:16; 15:9-17
Hebrews 10:19-22**

56. Life Squeeze

The dark ceiling swallowed mountaintops, squeezing plane and pilot toward rocks below. No flying over or around them today. Fickle clouds behind closed off returning home. Navigating the twisting rolls and folds between hills remained the only open path. "No problem," he assured himself, reciting memorized mantra. "Slow the airplane to eighty knots. Lower flaps to twenty degrees. Complete the checklist."

He found the one correct valley. It required flight at 5,500 feet or higher to clear the route. That also put him just below the angry roof. He snuggled the plane right, close to the canyon wall. That gave maximum room on the left for an escape turn.

In here, senses lied. What looked like level flight might actually be descent, climb, or turn. His eyes flicked to the instruments then back outside. More power needed to maintain altitude would reveal a downdraft pushing him towards the ground. But less power meant an updraft lifting him into peak-obscuring clouds. Look outside to avoid smashing into jagged crags. Look inside to learn the truth.

Sometimes life squeezes us toward rocky horror devoid of escape. Instinct screams, "Pull up, you fool!" Yet, even then, looking to quiet truth while keeping a wise eye on jutting destruction reveals a way out—no matter how convoluted.

So, what happened the last time you didn't yield to fear but trusted Him all the way through the maze to sun lit plains on the other side?

**Psalm 9:10; 20:1-8   John 16:12-15   Proverbs 1:32-33
1 Corinthians 10:1-13**

57. Two Flavors

Order exists in two flavors—natural and Divine. Natural order runs down. Observation reveals creation's beginning—a single, hot birthing point for matter, energy, space, and time nicknamed "The Big Bang." Since then, the universe dissipates, expanding faster and faster. Eventually, everything—galaxies, stars, planets, people and flowers—will dissolve, leaving only dark nothing, frozen at absolute zero (about −460°F.) We see it every day. Systems degrade from higher levels of order to lower. Coffee gets cold. Shoes wear out. Airplanes exhaust their fuel. Farms turn to weeds.

Even without studying physics, we intuitively fight against entropy. Unfortunately, nature's laws defeat our struggle. We can control our movement through space to a small degree—walking to the store or flying to Mars are roughly equivalent on a cosmic scale. But time defies us. We're just along for the ride. Though we try hard, every effort that seems right to us ends the same way. Our works evaporate. Death and corruption claim us.

God's order, on the other hand, grows. With neither beginning nor end, His Kingdom exists outside of space, excludes death, and lives free of the curse. Everywhere is here. All times are now. The deeper we go, the bigger it gets. Humility breeds kings, submission becomes power. Small seeds grow into immense trees; tiny faith relocates mountains. Spirit trumps letter, while mercy swallows judgment and fruit surpasses works. What sounds too good to be true, He exposes as understatement.

But when we forget why the Lord placed us here (or quit in disgust), Paul reminds us that, "I consider that our present sufferings are not worth comparing with the glory that will be revealed in us. The creation waits in eager expectation for the sons of God to be revealed. For the creation was subjected to frustration, not by its own choice, but by the will of the one who subjected it, in hope that the creation itself will be liberated from its bondage to decay and brought into the glorious freedom of the children of God."

So, how do you find yourself swimming against nature's current these days?

Ecclesiastes 2:4-11   Romans 8:18-21   Matthew 5:1-10
Revelation 21:6-7   Luke 9:46-48

58. Little Pawn

The pilot scanned the jungle a mile below. Flat, almost featureless, it stretched ahead like an endless emerald sea, fading into the eastern haze. Behind him, frozen waves of green hills mounted ever-higher assaults against snow-covered peaks. It seemed a primordial, liquid creature that occupied either a different space and time or, perhaps, his own world as he should have known it really to be.

The similarity to water unnerved him. A forced landing there could be bad. A plane could float on water. Life rafts offered a chance at survival. But the jungle offered no place to stand, no way to swim. Instead, it swallowed whatever dropped into it, digesting it beyond recognition or recall.

Sometimes, our foundation rebels. Our support threatens to consume us. Solid ground dissolves to morass, ever changing, never sure. We, like Korah's family, feel the little pawn falling in someone else's big game. Fortunately, the rock we barked our shin upon also provides firm footing against doubt's biggest waves.

So, what happened the last time you suddenly remembered "… that he who began a good work in you will carry it on to completion …"?

Numbers 16:1-35 1 Corinthians 10:1-4 Matthew 21:42-44 Philippians 1:3-6 Romans 9:30-33

59. Salt and Light

Salt of the earth—the edible rock—preserves food, enhances flavor, balances body fluid, and circulated as Roman money. God required it in grain offerings and used it to seal covenants and heal bad water.

Light of the sky—both particle and wave—the fastest we know, displaces darkness and shows the world. God created it first, called it good, and then used it to describe Himself.

Now, Jesus raises us dead ones up in order to show the riches of His grace. He calls us "salt of the earth" and names us "light of the world." Salt and light; season and shine. Always active, never hiding, He dispatches salt to cure hurt and reconcile man to God. He transmits light to reveal truth and conquer black lies.

But the enemy saps our spice and covers our flame, beguiling us until we drowse content to pass through life as a comfortable shadow.

So, when was the last time you touched that passion that God shut up in your bones?

2 Chronicles 16:7-9   John 8:12   Isaiah 40:28-31
2 Corinthians 5:16-21   Matthew 5:13-16

60. Daily Constraints

Sometimes we feel like grist, ground between the stones of life. What used to be fun isn't anymore. We call flying and playing with 300 horsepower engines "work." The joy of our child's birth hides in a fog of menus that turn into meals that turn into red hands pushing stacks of dirty dishes through soapy bleach water. The slow cycle of days morphs into speeding months that leave our dreams in a heap along with the ironing or hidden under the pile of unanswered letters.

What happened to the "seeking His Kingdom first" part of life so that "all this other stuff would be added"? Who has time to be spiritual?

The truth is that the Greeks were wrong. One of God's delightful mysteries is that our faithfulness to the constraints of daily life prepares us for eternity. The material world is not an inferior distraction. It's a part of God's creation that He calls good.

So, when your 13th landing of the day blurs with your 2nd, or when you know you've been picking up dirty socks forever, how does He remind you that you're still serving Him and advancing His Kingdom?

**Genesis 1:1-31   Luke 12:42-48; 16:10-12   Matthew 6:28-34
1 Peter 4:7-11**

61. The Straight Path

We laud order. Vertical walls, level floors, and square doorframes make the craftsman's reputation. Clear proposals mark the honest merchant. Full disclosure labels the trustworthy leader. Direct speech seems right, wholesome, and godly. We western believers in particular point authoritative fingers at "let your yes be yes and your no be no." We expect both church and consecrated life to base logical design upon rational strategy. Ought to be simple, right? Plan your flight then fly your plan.

Unfortunately, life is messy. People lose vision, fail to deliver, jump to conclusions, assume the worst, and disappoint at crucial moments. Simple living morphs into Byzantine labyrinths, swallowing participant and bystander alike. Later, when the kids sleep and cool, night wind blows in cricket sounds around our lone lamp, we wrestle despair, watching clean rot into quagmire. How can Jesus advance His kingdom using the church—a motley menagerie of rebels, malcontents, and stiff-necked prima donnas? What happened to the straight paths He promised if we committed our way to Him?

Depends upon what we mean by straight. Light, for example, always travels in a straight line. Yet, shine a ray near something really big with lots of gravity, such as Jupiter or the Sun, and it bends like wet spaghetti. Contradiction? No. Large mass distorts space itself so that the twisted only looks straight. Likewise, the fallen world's mass of sin only makes our perverted ways look upright. What we call straight—predictable, easy to follow and, above all else, controllable—leads to dark ways and the grave.

The measure of God's straight, on the other hand, rests in a different realm. Isaiah pointed at a voice of one calling, "In the desert prepare the way for the Lord; make straight in the wilderness a highway for our God. Every valley shall be raised up, every mountain and hill made low; the rough ground shall become level, the rugged places a plain. And the glory of the Lord will be revealed, and all mankind together will see it. For the mouth of the Lord has spoken."

So, when you look back at the craggy, crooked path He's led you along and consider the uncertain, hidden way ahead, how do you see it as a straight highway in His Kingdom pointing directly at Jesus?

Proverbs 3:5-6; 16:25   John 14:25-27   Isaiah 40:1-5
1 Corinthians 15:33   Matthew 5:33-37

62. Get Up!

Elias hung, trapped in thick darkness that clung without touch. He couldn't say if he stood, sat, or lay. Shivering without motion, he pushed against bonds but found none. Of course, he realized. He had nothing to push with. But at least his head stopped hurting. Then he remembered.

He hired himself out to build a house. "The finest in Nain," they said. How his mother's eyes glowed when he told her. Food, real food again, the first since father's death.

Death? He recalled clinging to a rope, high on the inside wall. He hammered at the stubborn roof timber. Crack! A glimpse of a falling beam, the surprise of sharp pain, and then nothing. Where was he? Cold invaded, searched, then pierced deep, aiming for his soul. Icy fingers snatched and tossed him into an endless pit.

Suddenly, a voice commanded, "Young man, I say to you, get up!" The darkness trembled then disintegrated into brilliance. He lay on his back, puzzled a moment at cloudless sky then snapped upright. A crowd of wide eyes and open mouths stepped back a pace.

"What are you looking at? How did I get here?"

No one answered, but a man said to his red-eyed mother, "Here is your son."

So, what happened the last time the Lord met you on the way to bury your final hope?

Luke 7:11-16   Acts 2:22-41   John 11: 17-43

63. Sticks and Stones

Sticks and stones may break my bones, but words will never hurt me. Baloney.

Thick armor and quick ducking deflect limb and rock. But words quickly pierce. Even ensconced hearts remain defenseless. Harsh words stir up anger. Many words invite sin. Smooth words seduce. Fool's talk brings a rod. Talk supplanting action leads to poverty. Gossip betrays a confidence then divides brothers. On the other hand, the wise know to hold their tongues until the joy of aptly spoken words shines like golden apples set in silver. A kind word cheers while a timely word brings good. And of course, a gentle answer turns away wrath.

What makes sound waves so potent? Force of personality? Magic? Hardly. The Word created the beginning and made us in His image. He entrusts each of us with a bit of His creative power. "Speak my word," He commands. "Administer my grace," He directs. "Whatever you bind and loose on earth will be touched in heaven," He promises. "Go ahead, tell the mountain to move," He counsels. He makes the point clear. Words contain His power, distinguishing bone from marrow, always accomplishing His purpose. Misused words hurt, divide, and destroy, but His words give life. Wrong speaking traps us in sin, but we escape by confessing that sin.

What's the trick to speaking the truth in love? The gift of freewill dictates that the privilege of power also requires the exercise of choice. Turns out, He offers two options. First, in the heat of daily battle, ask Him to set a guard over our mouth. Then, for life's long haul, He reveals that "out of the overflow of the heart the mouth speaks. The good man brings good things out of the good stored up in him, and the evil man brings evil things out of the evil stored up in him."

So, how do your words surprise you by revealing your heart?

Psalm 141:3   John 1:1; 1:14; 17:14-7
Proverbs 10:19-21; 15:1; 25:11   Romans 10:5-13
Matthew 12:33-37

64. High Ideals

Flying 35,000 feet over the Rockies at dawn, corduroy rows of cloud extend in orderly streets below. Mists cling to jutting mountain peaks, forcing wind aside into tumbling turbulence. That hurly–burly air torments us lower-altitude pilots. But up here, sipping coffee under cobalt sky, the shredded clouds below offer only artistic distraction. No thrashing about, fighting for control, banging head against window, or smacking cabin overhead. Clearly, it's better up high—smooth and easy to take the long view of life.

Life? That's the rub. God sends us to people. And they live in the tangled canyons below. A safe landing down there demands concentration. We configure the aircraft then adjust power, pitch, and rudder to arrive at our chosen touchdown spot on the airstrip. The closer we approach, the tougher it gets. The last few feet allow no error.

High ideals say life ought to stretch out smooth, clean, and simple. But real life gets messy up close, slapping the unwary off course. A harsh word breaks a marriage. A forgotten promise alienates a child. A debate splits a church. It seems like nothing works. Is life so impossible? Most certainly. Fortunately, we don't navigate the badlands on our own. The same One who walked on water makes every rough place plain.

So, what happened the last time you stumbled upon Jesus' footprints in the wilderness?

**Psalm 119:140   Matthew 25:34-45   Proverbs 15:1
John 6:16-21; 16:33**

65. Real Air

Jonah gagged, pulled slime from his mouth, then lay still in the sand. Panting hard, gulping his first real air in three days, he wallowed in half-digested flesh, bone splinters, and gritty muck that violated every pore. Blazing glare pierced his eyes. Bit by bit, first with fingers then with hands, he dragged himself away from the sea. His vision cleared a little and he focused on scarlet rivulets running across his white, bleached skin. Well, I'm alive enough to bleed, he mused in stupor. Then he remembered why.

Jesus says we're stuck on earth until He removes us. But He also says we citizens of His Kingdom don't belong here. So, what's the deal? Do we walk on earth with feet or in heaven with heart? Depends on what we want. If on earth alone, feet run and play —he world's a fun place. But then starving heart withers, separates, and dies. If in heaven alone, heart runs and hides—the world's a dark place. But then unguided feet drag across life, ignore King, and abandon lost sheep.

For the consecrated, He reveals a third way—do both. No joining the world, but no hiding from it, either. Instead, He says put feet made for walking to ground, and anchor heart made for seeing in heaven. Then, His Word lights the dark paths, reveals highways where none exist, and shines on rivers flowing in parched deserts.

So, when was the last time He gave you His perspective on what you despise?

**Jonah 1:1 – 2:10   Acts 1:8   Psalm 119:105   Romans 12:2
John 17:6-18   1 Corinthians 5:9-11**

66. Love Letters

If God wanted to reach us, how would He do it? He might speak directly—unless we were deaf. He might paint pictures—unless we were blind. He might write a book—unless we couldn't read. Or He could send a note.

But what kind of stationery would He use? Stone costs a fortune to mail; it scratches the furniture and renders many languages poorly. Surely He'd choose something better, something that received ink without smear, transported easily, and conveyed every nuance of His intent.

It turns out that for His most important correspondence, He uses only the best. For His most passionate love letters, He uses only the costliest material. He designs each tablet for its own unique communication. Some He fashions for wooing, others He makes for consummation. Some He molds for direction, and a few He crafts for the most difficult message of all—trust when none can rescue.

The other morning a living epistles said, "Unbelievers need to see us suffer with the same things they suffer, but with the hope they lack."

So, what happened the last time your calamity cast brilliant light into someone's dark corner?

Psalm 3:1-4   2 Corinthians 1:3-7; 3:1-3   Romans 12:1-2
Hebrews 2:10-18; 11:32-38   1 Corinthians 12:1-11

67. Vision

Birth of a vision: Moses hears God's call to help his people. Death of a vision: Moses acts, but defeat consumes promise, and he flees. Rebirth of a vision: God resurrects the dead dream and sends Moses back to Egypt. Testing of a vision: Moses acts again, but defeat consumes expectation, and his people reject him.

Perhaps Abraham spun myths. Maybe Jacob told tales. But Moses heard God, didn't he? Who can mock his doubt as he watched deliverance sink backwards? One author claims that true God seekers live in confusion. Why can't God speak simple instructions that achieve stated goals? He promises us the impossible and out of reach. But despite faith, nothing happens. Our failure either shouts that we missed God's will, or its whisper encourages us to wait for the invisible. What makes it so hard to tell the difference?

Two handicaps obstruct our sight: First, we believe we control reality. Second, we think linearly. Everything occurs in order; every cause generates an effect. Lay a foundation, place the walls, and only then add the roof because we know roofs don't hang in mid air. Sounds reasonable, except for one happy detail. God works differently. Knowing all ends before every beginning, He needs neither walls to support roofs nor causes to bring about effects.

On the other hand, if we fallen creatures can discern His thoughts, fathom His ways, and understand Him, what sort of God are we following, anyway? If we know what He knows, then He knows no better than we do. Scary thought. Fortunately, the dream-Giver fulfills our vision by offering Himself as our hope.

So, when was the last time you recounted the steps from your visions' burning bushes to their certain exodus out of slavery?

**Psalm 50:1-15   Acts 7:2-35   Isaiah 46:10   Romans 8:1-16
Matthew 11:25-28**

70

68. The Great Unknown

The student pilot stared at the compass. Alternate foot taps on right and left rudder pedals kept the assigned heading in place. "Got it!" he congratulated himself.

"Watch your altitude," the instructor admonished.

Altitude? The student's brow tightened—200 feet low and descending. He eased the wheel back, remembering pressure rather than gross movement.

"Let's keep an eye on the heading," the instructor reminded.

Heading? The unnoticed left turn had already taken them thirty degrees off course.

The instructor comforted, "Don't worry, you'll learn. You can't see most of what's happening now."

Indeed. In the mountains below, hidden birds flew, hunting secret food—unsuspecting worm and quivering rabbit. Trees sprouted, grew, died, and fell before no human audience. The air around him migrated a slow circle about the invisible low-pressure center, which, in turn, yielded to the Coriolis force of the spinning Earth. Above him radiation from unnamed stars smashed into high-flying oxygen molecules, scattering atomic debris over deserts, ridges, and valleys, untouched by shod-foot for a thousand years. And those stars, along with our sun, orbited the Milky Way galaxy's center every 220 million years or so.

We believe that our perception encompasses all the important parts of reality; yet the truth is most of creation carries on without our permission, knowledge, or imagination. As Jesus said, "The wind blows wherever it pleases. You hear its sound, but you cannot tell where it comes from or where it is going. So it is with everyone born of the Spirit."

So, what happened the last time the Lord flabbergasted you with how far He reached, how long He pursued, and how deeply He delved—all on your behalf, and all completely unknown to you?

Job 38:1-41   1 Corinthians 2:6-16   John 3:8

69. Contingency Plan

Professional aviators plan each flight confident of success, but at the same time also expect the worst to pounce and devour the unguarded. They memorize emergency checklists for engine failure on takeoff or fire in flight or landing with a flat tire or getting lost. The best always ask, "What's the backup plan?" Their confident doubting makes commercial aviation the world's safest transportation. And, therefore, we might reason that if contingency planning works so well in the air, it ought to serve the rest of life with equal benefit. Depends.

On one hand, the Bible counts the five virgins wise that brought extra oil and chides five foolish girls for bringing none. Praise comes to the diligent worker who stores up food for the winter, but hunger plagues the lazy man. It commends Joseph's famine backup plan and says to count the cost before going to war—can you go the distance or not? On the other hand, it chastises Nabal for keeping food for his own household rather than giving it to a brigand. It faults Judah for seeking allies when confronting vast armies and denounces the rich man for building bigger barns. Confusing?

We ask, "If this or that happens, then what?" What do we fall back on? Make a plan, or hope for the best? Wise stewardship of creation demands a backup plan. Creation, however, proves a poor foundation. Truly complete plans rest solidly on the Creator Himself. What was Esther's backup plan if the king withheld his scepter? What was Gideon's backup plan when he attacked the Midianites? What was the widow's backup plan when she gave her last two coins? The most solid possible—they stood on the Rock.

So, how did the Lord deliver you the last time that you, like Jonathan, showed yourself to the Philistines?

**Judges 7:1-21   Matthew 25:1-13   Esther 4:15-16
Mark 12:41-44   1 Samuel 14:1-13; 25:2-44**

70. Second Edge

The new Forest Service pilot looked again at the grass airstrip, 2,000 feet below. Tucked in tight between the river and two parallel ridges it looked right-sized for the Piper Cub parked there. For 20,000 pounds of a lumbering DC3, however, the mountain airport on his left looked anything but useable.

He glanced right, checking the instructor for any clue —a raised eyebrow, a forward lean—anything that said he'd take over now. The veteran pilot fiddled with his watchband. The student swallowed, understanding the message.

He slowed the big airplane and lowered the wheels. Already cramped by the valley walls, he descended another 1,000 feet. The only route passed through a narrow gap between the high rim on the right and a lower hill on the left. He squeezed through the slot, then turned a half-circle left, and lined up with the runway. Not much room, but practice with the airplane paid off. He pushed the wheel forward to plant the tires on the sod, started hard braking, and lowered the tail to the ground. He grinned as they stopped halfway up the 3,800-foot strip.

Desire grows to skill. Then, sweat hones that ability to a sharper, second edge. Finally, the true professional emerges. What do we do when it feels good to be really good? Take it as our earned right? Or stuff it down and beg forgiveness for pride? The truth is, God plants desire-producing gifts. The trick to successful application is offering all the fruit back to Him.

So, what happened the last time you had no idea how to accept praise for a job well done?

Genesis 22:1-19   2 Timothy 2:14-15   Proverbs 22:29
John 15:5   Ecclesiastes 10:10

71. Walking in the Open

"Maybe, I picked a bad time to start a fight, after all." Jonathan peered through a gap between boulders at the Philistine outpost atop the cliff high above. After his attack days ago, the enemy retaliated with vengeance. His father's army fled. Thousands deserted. The remnant army trembled in caves and crags. "I really thought this would go differently."

"What can we do?" his armor-bearer asked. "No one in our army has a single spear or sword except you and the King."

Fair question, Jonathan admitted, nodding slightly, biting his lower lip. "We can't do anything," he confessed.

The young man slumped, sighed, and wondered how much death hurt.

"But," Jonathan continued, suddenly resolute in new clarity, "our God can. Come, let's go over to the outpost of those uncircumcised fellows. Perhaps the Lord will act in our behalf. Nothing can hinder the Lord from saving, whether by many or by few."

They stood, walked into the open, and waited. Philistines quickly spotted them and shouted down, "Come on up, Hebrew pigs, and we'll teach you a lesson."

"Ah ha!" Jonathan said, grinning to his armor-bearer. "Climb up after me; the Lord has given them into the hand of Israel." They scaled the cliff, hand and foot, up to their tormentors. At the top, Jonathan drew sword, his armor-bearer wielded staff. They killed nearly two-dozen men, and panic struck the whole Philistine army.

God assigns a task. We rightly ask Him to supply, but then demand guarantees. We want everything firmly in our own hands before confronting the challenge. And what happens if we get our way? Do we pass test or gain victory? Do we learn trust or grow beyond comfortable ability? No, we simply manage what we already control. Just as we strengthen muscles only by first breaking them down, we acquire faith only by pushing past the limits of our understanding.

So, what did you learn the last time you saw fear disguised as prudence and control masquerade as good stewardship?

1 Samuel 14:1-14   Colossians 2:23   Psalm 119:130
1 Corinthians 3:18-20   Proverbs 3:5

72. Most Direct Way

At first the breeze over the stern refreshed, so without command they all raised and stowed oars. The sail snapped once and filled as Peter tightened the line, shaping the canvas belly. The water swished a quiet song to accompany the evening's last sun. Each man settled back into his favorite place, glad for respite from labor and heat. Jesus curled up on the aft bench and quickly fell asleep.

Later that night, the wave leapt from the dark, smashed into the starboard bow, and spun the boat halfway around to the left. Wind howled in concert, ripping away one corner of the sail; the rest flapped useless in sudden gale. Shouts punctuated awakened hands grasping for oar, rope, and tiller. Control almost regained, the wind shifted, and the boat lurched over onto its left side. Even larger waves converged from fore and aft, lifted the drenched craft high between them, then dropped it down a nearly vertical face. The bow plunged deep, barely surfacing just as another wave hit from the left.

Surging water inside the boat tangled flotsam with crying men, impotent against the triumphant squall. "Another like that, and we're dead—Bail!" Peter shouted then fell back, swept off his feet. The frenzied lake heaved from every direction and poured in, engulfing their last hope. And then, they saw Him in the back. Still asleep.

"Rabbi!" they cried out. "Don't you care that we're drowning?"

Jesus opened his eyes, yawned, stood up, and looked around. Chaos poised for final victory, ready to claim them all. "Quiet! Be still!" he commanded. Immediately, the water flattened and the wind vanished.

Sometimes, creation's convulsions obscure truth's straight path: "Let's go over to the other side." But God's word always follows Heaven's most direct route to accomplish His purpose, making straight highways in our wilderness.

So, what happened the last time Jesus opened a way for you where none could exist?

**Proverbs 3:5-6   Mark 4:35-41   Isaiah 55:10-11
2 Corinthians 4:16-18**

73. Just You and Me

We North Americans stand, single file, patiently waiting our turn. No service for number two until the cashier finishes number one. Makes sense to us, but others call such passive delay stupid. Why wait when pushing gets faster service? We point out, correctly, that God set up an orderly creation. Effects require causes, consequences need actions, future grows only from past. No cutting in line; nothing may come before Him. We know that if we seek Him first, He'll add everything like vine feeding branch.

However, facing the living God scares us. We have to hate spouse, progeny, and our own lives in comparison to Him. He asks hard things, but the ancients' painful lessons impress us. Wood's just wood. Stone's just stone. Who's dumb enough to talk to dead stuff? No kneeling to statues. No offering to idols. "Just You and me, Lord," we proclaim. "No one else, but You," we affirm.

Indeed. The truth is, our heart's secrets stand in first place. What threat worries us? What loss horrifies us? What lust motivates us? What dream beguiles us? Fortunately, our jealous God permits nothing to separate us from Himself. He neither coddles our infatuations nor indulges our fears. He grants us freedom to reap their harvest until frustration, perplexity, desperation, or terror persuades us to release our grip and allow His perfect love to drive the idols out.

So, what did you learn the last time He peeled your heart open to reveal your own pet elephant at the head of the line?

**Matthew 22: 36-40   2 Corinthians 6:14-18   Romans 8:31-39
Galatians 6:7-10**

74. Small and Quiet

The crowd swelled, clamoring to glimpse the lame man dance. A thousand eyes followed every exuberant leap—arms thrown high, hands splayed wide. Whooping shameless joy, the beggar skipped circles around Peter and John. Peter asked the gawkers, "Men of Israel, why does this surprise you? Why do you stare at us as if by our own power or godliness we had made this man walk?"

So, what surprises us about God's power? That it exists? That it works? No, we admitted some time ago that His power exceeds ours. We preach about it moving in our lives. We talk about it working on Earth. We tell its stories to kids. More adventurous souls even pray to receive a generous glop to energize a calling.

Unfortunately, we search much, but find little. We decry our churches' lack, and long for the abundant flow of robe and sandal days. And some of us—secretly, of course—wonder if miracle tales aren't metaphors after all. Like the crowd, we assume that if we name something, we also understand it. Those folks looked for a magician to beat Romans. We look for wonders to fix country and culture. Both remain disappointed.

The truth is, we often miss the Holy Spirit when he jumps out, blocks our way, and thumbs his nose at us. We expect big and flashy and filter out small and quiet.

So, what happened the last time you heard God speak through an acquaintance of lesser esteem?

Psalms 8:1-9   1 Corinthians 1:18-31   Acts 3:1- 26   2 Timothy 3:1-5

75. Even the Turkeys

Voices? Peter, mostly asleep, weighed the value of looking. Only the four of them climbed up here. So, who were these new voices, these different voices? Curiosity defeated slumber, one lid lifted a slit. Blinding light pierced. He snapped fully awake, up on feet then down to knees. Intense radiance—painful yet enthralling—drew him to ... to ... Jesus? Yes! Unmistakably him, but Someone else, too. Who was this Being, shining and glorious, known but terrifying and unimaginable even though seen? The man proclaiming Jesus as the Christ eight days earlier, truly saw His Lord for the first time.

Likewise, we no longer regard Jesus from a worldly point of view. Overwhelmed by rescue, awed by power, humbled by love, we gratefully accept the ambassador's commission—the ministry of reconciliation. But bringing the world into agreement with Jesus immediately forces confrontation with those who make up the world. It gets hard to remember that the person we see only dimly resembles who God made him. We get over dismissing the truly disadvantaged—not their fault, after all. Then, we learn that God loves people from the weird cultures, too. But what about jerks, those who act stupidly, regardless of race, gender, religion, creed, or national origin? Eventually we get it; God cherishes even the turkeys.

However, even after regarding no one else from a worldly point of view, we still resist seeing ourselves as He does. The less honest fear His dominion. The more honest doubt His grace. Either way, we impede His appeal of reconciliation through us. We forget the truth that "I have been crucified with Christ and I no longer live, but Christ lives in me."

So, what happened the last time you realized that the old was gone and that you were, indeed, a new creation?

**Matthew 17:1-8   Galatians 2:20   2 Corinthians 5:11-21
Ephesians 4:20-24**

76. Great Sin

Hazael stared, open-mouthed at the man before him. The Jewish defier of kings, the worker of miracles, the mighty mouthpiece of God, shook, hands over face, weeping like a woman.

"Sir, why do you weep?"

"Because I know the harm you will do to the Israelites," Elisha answered. "You will set fire to their fortified places, kill their young men with the sword, dash their little children to the ground, and rip open their pregnant women."

"How could I ever do such a great thing?" Hazael asked, amazed. "I don't have that kind of power."

Clearly a magnificent accomplishment in that ancient officer's eyes, but today we rank it atrocity and dismiss it as the proclivity of a primitive culture. If that's so, why then do we condemn adultery, but justify anger? Prosecute embezzlement, but wink at avarice? Punish murder, but ignore resentment? If we grade sin to mark our progress towards righteousness, does refraining from enough bad stuff makes us good?

So, what happened the last time you realized that your minor flaws branded you a gross sinner in your host culture's eyes?

**2 Kings 8:9-14 Ephesians 2:8-10 Matthew 5:21-30
Romans 3:9-18; 7:14-25**

77. The Leap

David's nose, numb after seven days pressed against stone, still smelled grit blown by pleading breath. "My God, my God. Don't let my guilt fall on this child. Punish me, not the innocent," he repeated continuously, cracked lips touching the mucus-wet floor. He willed his words through the solid tiles beneath scrapped forehead, bruised knees, and aching toes. All the promise, all the hopes gone, destroyed because he failed ... He, defeater of giants, deliverer from Philistines, lay prostrate, felled by his own desire. A woman tricked Samson, but he, God's anointed king to Israel, chose destruction himself. "Oh God, spare the boy, take me." Imagined scenes flashed through his mind—running to roof's edge and before servants could react, hurling himself off. Or grabbing a guard's sword, falling on it, and finally receiving what he had inflicted on the Lord's enemies—as he was now. Even as he pleaded, a plan formed, ready for the right moment ...

Complete failure smashes us against the rock of decision. Hide in our defeat, or cling to God's mercy? Wallow in condemnation, or embrace the Spirit's conviction? Demand our right to self-destruction, or surrender to His claim on our soul? One path exalts us; the other glorifies Jesus. Bad deeds do not repel goodness. Good deeds do not attract mercy. Rather, the Lord sends them following after us all the days of our lives.

So, what happened the last time crushing defeat forced you to choose between flying into self-pity or leaping off the cliff of His grace?

2 Samuel 17:13-23   Romans 5:15-17; 8:1-17   Psalm 23:1-6
1 Corinthians 7:23

78. No Two Alike

Why do they sing choruses/hymns? What's wrong with hymns/choruses?

Why do they build cathedrals/shacks? What's wrong with simplicity/honor?

Why do they stand/sit during worship? What's wrong with sitting/standing?

Why do they ignore/demand time? What's wrong with punctuality/relationship?

Why do they dress up/dress down for church? What's wrong with comfort/class?

Why do they have long/short statements of faith? What's wrong with grace/correctness?

Why do they sit like stones/jump like clowns? What's wrong with participation/reverence?

God creates us like snowflakes, no two alike. Then, He broadcasts us throughout creation like sea's sand or night's stars. Such abundance mixed with freewill yields nearly infinite variety. So, why is it that, even as we revel in divine freedom, we also despise freedom's fruit?

What happened the last time you discovered that your hokey was someone else's holy?

**Genesis 22:15-18   2 Corinthians 5:16   Romans 14:1-23
Galatians 3:26-29**

79. Beautiful Feet

She gave up trying to stop. No stranger to strange men in strange houses, she stood behind him as he reclined at the crowded banquet table. Noiseless sobs, rising from unknown depths, shook her slender frame. Twin streams surged past long, vainly clenched eyelashes, falling, splashing, etching pale rivulets across his grime-encased feet. As she opened her eyes, the pent-up reservoirs poured out, making a muddy mess. Kneeling quickly, she loosed flowing hair to clean ankles, toes, sole, and heel. Then, leaning lower, she kissed the feet that brought such good news.

She didn't know why she came or why she stayed, weeping and cleaning. She was accustomed to being the object of desire. But now, perhaps fearful of publicly admitting interest in her beauty and ability, no one acknowledged her presence. Except him. His words in town earlier that day pierced deep until she gladly admitted the truth about herself. Everyone else in town, of course, already knew who she was, what she was. His gaze, also knowing, displayed neither distain nor rejection. Instead, it called her a princess, bright and clean. Who in the world did he think she was?

That elusive love for one another—touted as the sure sign we belong to Him—begins with regarding each other from the Creator's viewpoint, not the creation's. Natural eyes, designed for life inside creation's cage, see only the natural man. But, heart's eyes, designed for heaven's life, see the King's image bearer. The trick? Choose to believe before seeing rather than after. Faith draws impossible beauty out of ugly souls.

So, what happened the last time you treated a bother like a brother?

Isaiah 52:7   John 13:34-35   Matthew 5:43-48
2 Corinthians 5:16-21   Luke 7:36-50

80. Overcomers

The Program Manager sighed, head in hands. Late Friday afternoon sunlight streamed across the open letter on his desk. Monday morning, the government agency said, the avgas price would triple—retroactive six months. Above it, the computer displayed his boss's email. Effective immediately, the entire region was under a ten percent budget cut. He tried to reply, but rats gnawed the server cable again, dropping them offline. The technician could fix it —when he returned from vacation.

"Later …" he declared, pushing himself up. They had to fly the doctor out of the jungle and to the capital. Tomorrow was his last chance to get out of the country. What a time for both aircraft to be in maintenance . The plane almost ready would have to wait. The part it needed languished in a car on the other side of a landslide. That meant working all night to get the second plane ready. And what about his wife's birthday dinner? He lifted the phone to cancel their first date in months, but heard no dial tone. Apparently, rodents dine on phone lines as well.

Some days even nature itself seems to conspire against us, echoing the foul broodings that still dribble from our soul's darker corners. Fortunately, the One who directed us to "Overcome barriers" also equipped us to obey His command to "Be overcomers." He sends us to jobs where nothing works, where jungles impede, where destruction threatens, and condemnation saps. We change from whiners to winners by getting over real obstacles, not fake.

The truth is, Jesus transforms us into overcomers to give us credibility to administer his grace to others.

So, what did you learn the last time you remembered that you will, indeed, see his goodness in the land of the living because everyone born of God overcomes the world?

Job 19:25-27   James 4:7   Luke 10:1-3; 18-20
1 John 5:1-5   John 16:33

81. Center of Gravity

Created things die—even stars. Some explode violently as novas. Some fade to white or brown dwarfs then fizzle to dark cinders. Some get dense. Normally, a star's fierce nuclear fire pushes outward just enough to prevent the gas from falling in. But when the star burns its last fuel, the crucial balance disappears. Billions of cubic miles of gas crash inward smashing the atoms together, forming a neutron star ten miles across. A teaspoon of its material weighs 100 million tons.

And some stars, starting with those about three times bigger than our sun, collapse their entire mass into black holes. These infinitely small points exert such tremendous gravitational influence that nothing escapes their pull—not even light. They become the center of their neighborhoods. Like gluttonous sharks swimming in quicksand they devour all within reach. What's farther away, they imprison into orbits around them.

Unlike stars, God gives us freewill. We establish the center of gravity for that portion of creation entrusted to our care. Make life's purpose about us, and nothing escapes, not even light. We suck others into decaying orbits that spiral down into old nature's death. But make life's purpose about Him, and He radiates every good thing, especially light. He lifts others into higher orbits, transforming them into His life. After all, "The mind of sinful man is death, but the mind controlled by the Spirit is life and peace ..."

So, what happened the last time you realized that your focus determined the nature of your influence?

**Proverbs 16:7   Romans 8:5-8   Matthew 5:13-16; 6:22-23
Jude 1:3-13   Luke 6:43-45**

82. Precious Treasure

"Gone! They're all gone!" he said through clenched teeth. "Every woman, every child—gone!" Dried, white channels ran down the ash-smeared faces around him. Their beards, soaked with too many tears, jerked short nods. In Ziklag's smoldering ruin, curse and wail sank to dark rage.

"We could've stopped the motherless pigs," he said grasping at a now useless sword. "If we'd have been here." Eyes narrowed, he went on, "But no! He had us off playing nice with those uncircumcised Philistines. It's his fault, and I say we make that son of a dog, that spawn of Jesse pay!" He squatted to grab a charred brick, but a dozen arms held him. Others, however, agreed, already clutching stones.

Meanwhile, David, weak with weeping, strengthened himself in the Lord.

The truth is that our enemy attacks everything we value—spouse and home, son and daughter, money and ministry, freedom and peace, time and good name. He lays waste the countryside, assaults the walls, ravages the courtyard, burns the storehouses, and then pierces deep for the throne itself.

So, what happened the last time you realized that a heart to please God ranked as your most precious treasure?

1 Samuel 30:1-25   1 Peter 5:8-9   John 10:7-10
1 John 3:21-24   1 Thessalonians 2:4

83. All Good Things

Committing our lives to God yields good things. He relieves our burdens, gives us daily bread, and supplies all our needs. He lifts us up on eagle's wings and sustains us when we can neither walk nor run. He binds up our broken hearts, frees us from captivity, and proclaims His favor. He comforts our mourning, adorns us with praise, and crowns us with beauty. He even rebuilds ancient ruins, restores devastation, and renews our dead lives.

Sometimes, though, we get stuck thinking "cause and effect." Do this; receive that. Ask for His help; succeed at His assigned task. Tithe on our income; pay all the bills. Ask for wisdom; receive His guidance. It does make sense, and He even commands us to ask for anything we want and expect everything we need.

But He neither lives in, nor limits His action to the good of creation's small spaces. Instead He offers the best and invites, "Walk with me." He presents the finest and counsels, "Apart from me you can do nothing." He recommends the greatest and promises, "He who unites himself with the Lord is one with him in spirit." In fact, He confesses that "He can do only what he sees His Father doing." Acting on His principles gives good, but clinging to Him immerses us in best.

So, what happened the last time you realized that only He, Himself, was your peace?

**Isaiah 40:27-31; 61:1-11   1 Corinthians 6:17   John 5:19-21
Ephesians 2:14-18**

84. Hiding

We pilots love sky life. That aerial in-between place draws us because it touches everywhere without being anywhere. It connects all human worlds yet remains aloof. Some of us even prefer its nether-world freedom to choose identity and control exposure. And winged-work demands such care, skill, and attention that our distance from mere mortals makes sense. We expend so much that we have nothing left for other worlds—or lives.

Propellers, housework, and Bible studies all offer great cover. Professional smoke—whether from aviator or housewife—deceives many. But the truth is that God asks us to live as who He made us, not as who we fear others expect. He created real people to administer His grace to others, not wraiths to walk across life's stage touching no one.

So, what happened the last time you used your God-given retreat to hide from His calling?

Matthew 5:13-16   Galatians 1:10   Mark 4:18-19
1 Peter 4:10   Luke 8:16-18

85. The Right Equipment

God equips us for every call. He gives creation-pieces to all who travel through mortal life. Fish receive fins and gills, horses sport hoofs, and birds come equipped with wings. We humans get bodies, strength, intelligence, ability, focus, affection, time, and money— each a tool designed for the job at hand. Roofs and clothes protect fleshly tents. Imagination births vision. Skill turns dreams into reality. It all works great until we start thinking like owners and congratulate ourselves on acquiring, achieving, and advancing.

Stewards, on the other hand, remember that we keep only existence and freewill. All the rest comes on loan for the short journey. Managerial skills, good looks, 2 x 4s, and certificates of deposit work fine here but not in heaven. Eventually, we return everything. The 10% tithe simply reminds us of who owns what — the other 90% is His too.

He showed us a long time ago that "You may say to yourself, 'My power and the strength of my hands have produced this wealth for me.' But remember the Lord your God, for it is he who gives you the ability to produce wealth, and so confirms his covenant, which he swore to your forefathers, as it is today."

So, what did you learn the last time you found that because of your best efforts, your abilities became liabilities, your strength turned to weakness, and your affections sank to addictions?

**Exodus 19:3-6   Galatians 4:1-2   Deuteronomy 8:10-18
Hebrews 13:20-21   Isaiah 64:6**

86. Not Fair

It doesn't seem fair. We have so much: safety, freedom, home, income, stuff, health, opportunities, choices. Most in the world don't. Guilt tempts us, but condemnation is dumb. Neither noble deed nor selfish scheme put us here. Our unique prosperity begs questions: How come we weren't born laborers with load-bent backs, unshod, toothless, old and spent at thirty? Are we smarter? Luckier? More deserving?

Then we read the requirement: those who receive a lot have to give a lot. Okay, equal trades make sense. But how much is enough? Until we reach the lowest common level? We know we can't buy salvation. Does God bill us for the rest? What if we can't pay?

The truth is, we own nothing and, therefore, owe nothing. Instead, He says, "Dispense the grace I put into your care" Sometimes He directs us to share a little, other times to give it all. Sometimes he asks us to employ it, other times to manage it well enough to employ others. Neither buyers nor sellers, we are, in fact, distributors of His goodwill, commanded to broadcast with flagrant abandon.

So, what sprang up around you the last time you truly appreciated your current abundance?

**Mark 10:29-31   1 Corinthians 4:7   Luke 12:48
2 Corinthians 9:6-15**

87. True Nature

Everything demonstrates its own nature. Water falls as rain, runs as rivers, rises as clouds, then falls again as snow. Snow packs to ice. Ice compresses into glaciers, slipping to the sea. Not stopping at water's edge, great chunks splash under then bob up to float away, housing seals and harassing ships, quietly melting back into the ocean from which they came.

But suppose water suddenly denied itself and imitated other liquids whose ice grows denser and heavier, rather than lighter. Now, the calving glacier drops monstrous icebergs that plunge beneath the waves and roll like boulders down slopes to the cold ocean floor. They pile thicker and higher, finally reaching the surface, leaving only a thin layer of liquid sloshing across seas of solid ice—no tides, no plankton, no oxygen, no life.

Unlike water, we get to choose our nature—human or divine. One chains us to the old man's sinking ship. The other transforms us into new creations who can do only what His nature dictates. The trick is unlocking the wild, abandoned passion He planted within us to trust Him for what only He can do.

So, what impossible, unrealistic dream to glorify Him crashes against the bars of your good sense?

Romans 8:1-17   2 Corinthians 9:8-9
Ephesians 2:1-10; 4:17-32   Philippians 4:13

88. Our Way

Lists lead to death,
But grace points to life.

Law demands strength,
But love requires surrender.

The old man chooses downfall
Rather than abdicate his throne.

The new man cedes his domain
Rather than risk missing the King.

So, what happened the last time you told the Lord you'd rather
do it your way?

Proverbs 14:12   John 15:13   Luke 19:1-10   2 Corinthians 3:4-6

89. Attracting Critics

Leaders attract critics. God sends leaders as "first in the attack and last in the retreat." He calls them, lifts them up, and exposes them as targets before friend and foe alike. He gives only anointing as the armor that welcomes a friend's criticism yet deflects a rebel's attack.

Followers straddle diverging paths. On one hand, God gives perception, intelligence, and freewill then says, "Go use them." He encourages submitted conflict, expects disagreement and glues us together with His love—even when we argue passionately.

On the other hand, He offers no compromise when talking of masters commanding and slaves submitting but simply reminds us of the earth swallowing Korah. How do we do both?

The truth is, He gives the whole truth to no one person but to the collective community. Some followers function as loyal opponents, revealing gaps in thinking and offering alternative perspectives, seeking God's glory through joint effort. Rebels, however, fail to recognize and submit to authority's source. Instead, bent on destruction, they strike for the heart and seek their own glory.

So, what happened the last time you realized how much of your rebellion His grace forgave?

**Numbers 16:1-35   Romans 2:5-11; 13:1-7   Matthew 18:23-34
Jude 1:3-16**

90. **Quiet River**

Come quiet river,
Awake O' sleeping stream.
Flow again,
Run again.
Let your meager trickle
Return to torrential blessing.
Grant parched valleys
Cascades of anointing.

The Holy Spirit bestows gifts so that we, in turn, administer God's grace. But sometimes we commandeer the privilege, calling it our possession instead. That packs muddy logs into tangled dams, blocking the current. Behind, stagnant water swells, but downstream everything in our assigned watercourse withers.

So, what happened the last time you admitted that your word alone could blast open the jam?

**Isaiah 41:17-20   James 1:26   Matthew 6:1-5
Revelation 22:1-2   John 7:37-38**

91. Tasting the Imminent

Moses squinted at sinking sun. Even late afternoon glare couldn't hide winding ribbons of rising dust. Spear points sparkled and helmets glinted against dancing silhouettes riding hard, speeding to the kill—still a long way off, yet already too close for escape along the coast. No place to defend or even hide here. Trapped between sea ahead and Egyptians behind, they were sheep awaiting ravenous wolves.

People surged, a living, crying sea themselves. "Was it because there were no graves in Egypt that you brought us to the desert to die? What have you done to us by bringing us out of Egypt? Didn't we say to you in Egypt, 'Leave us alone; let us serve the Egyptians?' It would have been better for us to serve the Egyptians than to die in the desert!"

"I brought you only where the Lord led. You've seen His hand just as I have," Moses answered.

"Why did you bring us here without knowing the way was open? We trusted you, but you lied to us!" they shouted.

His fingers closed around his long, wooden staff as a wild, crazy thought grew in his mind. "So, that's what you're about, Lord," he mused to himself. Then, looking up, he called out to the rock-bearing mob, "Do not be afraid. Stand firm, and you will see the deliverance the Lord will bring you today …"

God chose not to spare the Israelites stress by parting the Red Sea before they arrived. He ordered no scouts ahead to confirm open way or inspect water walls. He bypassed many useable roads to send them via the one impossible route. He waited until the Israelites tasted imminent death before destroying every enemy. He demonstrated no tolerance for the human security addiction or control lust. Instead, He demanded complete trust before deliverance, not after.

So, what happened the last time you realized that God's command to you comes with no guarantee that the path is visible, open, or even exists?

**Exodus 14:1-31   John 14:1   2 Chronicles 20: 20-22
1 Peter 2:6   Mark 5:36-43**

92. Right Water

The old tale tells of a sower spreading seed; with measured pace he crosses ready field. Hand dips to basket then flings to air, broadcasting harvest hope upon fickle ground.

Likewise, today we fancy ourselves Royal farmers, planting a word here, a testimony there. Some return a crop, but many do not. "Shallow dirt," we sigh. "Too many rocks," we observe. "Dang crows!" we complain.

But what happens when He names us the garden, when He plants His Words in us? Some germinate, but many sleep. Too many weeds? Bad soil? More likely, wrong water. Just as desert grass sprouts only in cold rain, so too Divine seed drinks only living water.

So, what happened the last time you found yourself drawing from the wrong well?

2 Kings 2:19-22   Mark 4:3-20   Jeremiah 2:13   James 1:21

93. Inner Access

We see a king in brilliant armor, leaping to the parapet, raising silver trumpet. His clarion blast echoes off forest and castle wall alike. Then, trading horn for shield, he lowers his helmet visor, raises a gleaming blade, and prepares to repel yet another onslaught of the hideous dragon hordes. Mighty in valor, steadfast in courage, defender of the realm since inception, he faces mortal foe knowing full well the price of failure.

The truth, on the other hand, reveals a leprous vagrant scuttling behind reeking mounds. Decaying refuse dampens his shrill squeaks. With frantic grasps, he pulls slimy cardboard over pocked face and clutches a rotting branch. He swings the crooked stick, blindly thrashing, whirling in ever widening circles, wailing, "Go away! Don't touch me! Leave me alone!" Like a warty toad, he hops about his tangled trash domain, squawking defiance at the Holy Spirit waiting patiently just beyond the moat.

We know that while the new man proclaims truth and confesses freely, the old man hides truth and deceives even himself. Replacing old with new ought to be simple. Unfortunately, though defeated, the old man remains perversely clever, sinking scores of fear's hooks into the heart. Our power can neither defeat him nor control him. Only Perfect Love snips the barbed points—if we allow the Lord access to our inner parts.

So, what happened the last time you realized just how long 'fear of man' had ensnared you?

**Isaiah 64:6   1 John:4:18   Proverbs29:25   Philippians 3:4-7
Romans 6:1-14**

94. Rich Sinners

The just and the unjust both require air.
The just and the unjust both crave water.
The just and the unjust both seek food.
The just and the unjust both need light.
The just and the unjust both get cold at night.
The just and the unjust both get wet in the rain.
The just and the unjust both strive to survive.
The just and the unjust both reflect the Creator's image.

If Christ sacrificed Himself to make us just while we were still unjust, does He now value us more? Does He, in fact, love the justified more than the sinner?

How did you feel the last time you noticed that He prospered Samaritans next door but left you broke?

**Matthew 5:43-48; 20:1-16   Romans 5:6-8   John 12:30-32
Colossians 3: 5-11**

95. Holding Heading

The panel vanished. Night invaded. Rain roared against fuselage. Turbulence smacked wings. He fumbled, found, and flicked on the flashlight, scanning the cabin. Gripping the light between his teeth and controls with his left hand, he obeyed the checklist. Methodical diligence revealed the truth. The engine worked fine, but no alternator output. No battery output. No electricity. No lights. No radios. No calling for help. Worse, no electronic beacon to follow. His warm cockpit throne, once adorned with control's glowing jewels, became just a bouncing seat, lost in the storm.

Then, he remembered. Neither seen nor heard, magnetic lines of force span the planet from pole to pole. So faint that only a tiny magnet suspended in liquid feels them, they, nonetheless, speak constant truth. He swung the pale white circle up to the compass. Dipping and bopping in the bumps, it still declared plain fact, "You're headed this way." Looking at the chart, he confirmed tonight's area of good weather, measured distance—yes, the gas would last—and calculated heading. Though blind, deaf, and alone in wild, midnight clouds, he turned left to head west. Eventually, he'd reach clear weather if he held this course.

Sometimes, our souls' dark nights hide everything. No one knows, no one sees, no one cares, nothing to hang onto, nothing to believe in, no goal, no purpose. Why bother? Yet, neither seen by eye nor heard by ear, His voice spans all creation and beyond. So faint that only a surrendered heart feels Him, He nonetheless is Truth. Often, in the worst raging maelstroms He counsels simply, "Hold this heading."

So, what happened the last time maintaining His invisible course rescued you from howling despair and brought you suddenly and unexpectedly back into His light?

**Psalm 119:105; 139:1-24   1 Corinthians 4:5   John 14:6-7
Hebrews 10:35-38**

96. Jesus Calls

Jesus calls, but sometimes we hear nothing.
Jesus calls, but sometimes we give no response.
Jesus calls, but sometimes we hear only what we desire.
Jesus calls whether we listen or not, always faithful, never stopping.

We call, and Jesus always hears.
We call, and Jesus always understands.
We call, and Jesus always replies.
We call, but sometimes Jesus responds in ways we neither recognize nor expect.

So, what happened the last time you sought His boon and found Him seeking you instead?

**Psalm 86:6-8   Luke 16:14-16   Proverbs 1:20-33
John 4: 23; 9:41; 15:16**

97. Dying Daily

Sometimes we believe that "dying daily" means rejecting what we want and embracing what we hate. If it tastes good, spit it out. If it looks good, close your eyes. If it sounds good, turn it off. If you like it, throw it away. If you want it, forget it. If it feels right, despise it. If you gain by it, give it away. If it satisfies, stop. If it pleasures, look for the devil. If it comforts pain and brings peace, standby—the hammer's about to fall.

Actually, beating poor "worm Jacob" misses the point entirely. Like trumpeted, street-corner prayer, abusing the soul entrusted to our care yields only its own reward. Camelhair coats itch, all right, but nothing more. Gaunt faces carried about by scruffy shoes impress only the undiscerning. The cunning usurper remains firmly on his throne despite blows and deprivation.

The fact is, God is good. He creates all good things. Authors all good thoughts. Designs all good plans. Paints all good sights. Composes all good sounds. Conceives all good purposes. Everything we call good springs from longing for Him—a desire He plants and cultivates. "Dying daily" means surrendering daily—surrendering our life's throne, surrendering our right to define our own good.

So, what happened the last time you lost a battle, and, despite your very best efforts to the contrary, His grace overwhelmed and invaded your kingdom?

**Isaiah 41:14   Romans 8:28-30   Luke 9:23-24
1 Corinthians 15:31   Acts 14:14-18**

98. Our Challenge

The Lord declares that He, Himself, is our high tower. "Flee to me!" He cries. "Hide in me!" He offers. "Take refuge in me!" He implores. Sounds good, but how do we run into something we can neither see nor touch? Some days it seems the harder we try, the worse it gets.

Unfortunately, we confuse His easy walk, complicate His simple life and convolute His straight path. We do know that the slightest lean towards Him draws Him rushing to us. But we also forget that the closer He gets to us, the farther we seem from Him. The better we see Him, the worse we look. And when we finally allow Him to touch us, two things happen: we see our complete depravity, and we receive our clearest revelation of Him.

If we listen, we hear, "You're beautiful. You're worthy. You're loved. You're desired. You're sought after. You're cherished. You're valued. You're important. Haven't I chosen you?" Our challenge? Accept it.

So, what happened the last time you hung on only in hope that He would notice your fingernails imbedded into His ankle?

Psalm 61:1-3   Luke 11:13   Proverbs 18:10; 30:5
Romans 15:13   John 3:16-17; 15:9-12; 16:33

99. Pay Up!

Shaking knees carried him from throne-room to hall to courtyard and out the palace gate. An hour before he walked in, dreading and leaden. Now, exuberant and light he skipped out. Then, full realization—not only spared from prison, slavery, and torture, the king's forgiveness also made him wealthy. He shuddered, still smelling disaster's fading stench, then shook his head. No more playing fast and loose. Careful, conservative, and controlled—that's the word. He smiled thinking of new possibilities.

Six weeks later, he strolled the portico of his new house. The setting sun's light wrapped each enlarged barn in gold. The wine press, though, he'd leave as is and, instead, build a second next to it to process two varieties of grapes at the same time. Better market penetration. He stepped down onto the gate path and saw a familiar shape skulking in the shadow. Yes, it was him! "Ahija?" he called out as he strode over, reached down and dragged the quivering man to his feet. "You scoundrel!" he shouted. "Pay me! Now!"

"But master," he pleaded. "I don't have it yet. Give me more time."

"You worthless piece of …" he spat, shaking the terrified servant's throat with both hands. "Guards!" he commanded to those already running towards the commotion. "Throw him into prison. And keep him there until he pays everything he owes."

Sometimes, as the Lord's deliverance and blessings settle in, we quickly grow accustomed to prosperity's fruit and lose sight of where, exactly, we stand. Our wealth's city provides solid footing to wield power. Our high walls create options. We know safety, security, and peace. Unfortunately, we often end up mistaking our ease for His blessing and our comfort for His favor. Desperate dependence upon the Lord's mercy, on the other hand, scares us like walking on thin ice or dancing at cliff's edge. Most often it seems that only His whim stays us just short of disaster.

The trick, of course, is to plunge our feet deeper until they anchor on The Rock—totally out of our control and understanding.

So, what happened the last time you realized you were trying to serve two different masters?

**Exodus 17:1-7   Matthew 18:23-35   Psalm 111:10
1 Corinthians 10:3-4   Proverbs 18:11**

100. Run

I: Jesus formed me.
CAN: Jesus drives out fear.
DO: Jesus created everything.
ALL: Jesus loses nothing.
THINGS: Jesus understands real life.
THROUGH: Jesus lives in me.
HIM: Jesus possesses all authority.
WHO: Jesus sits at Father's right hand.
STRENGTHENS: Jesus works in my weakness.
ME: Jesus knows where I live.

So, what happened that last time He asked you to run when you couldn't stand?

**Isaiah 40:31; 44:2   2 Corinthians 12:8-9   Matthew 28:18
Galatians 2:20   John 1:1-3   Hebrews 4:14-16   Luke 12:6-7
1 John 4:15-18   Romans 8:33-39**

101. Unfamiliar Paths

Sometimes fog wraps us—thick, close, and deep. Dim, dripping gray, not dark, yet revealing nothing. Ground and sky hide. Chasm and boulder lurk silently, preying on neglect. Alone, we shuffle, walking hobbled by straining eye's imagination. Path long gone, only our guess guides. Suddenly groping claws reach out. A bear? A dragon? No, just a tree, dead and twisted, matching empty heart. The black thoughts say, "I messed up and missed the way. It was a nice dream, but cruel ..."

On one hand, we know that circumstances distract us, our clever plans delude us, and coddled fear blinds us. They conspire, obscuring the land with dingy smoke and choking life with doubt's clinging tentacles. On the other hand, ankles twisted on sliding scree and foreheads smacked on granite shout with sharp, demanding reality. Pain, after all, hurts.

The trick is remembering that even truer than pain, He says, "I will lead the blind by ways they have not known, along unfamiliar paths I will guide them; I will turn the darkness into light before them and make the rough places smooth. These are the things I will do; I will not forsake them."

So, what happened the last time you were lost in the desert and found you hadn't even seen that stream of living water running beside you the entire way?

**1 Kings 17:1-6   Ezekiel 47:1-12   Isaiah 42:16; 44:21; 48:17-19
John 7:37-39   Jeremiah 2:13**

102. Don't You Care?

Martha pushed down and dough oozed up around red knuckles. Push and ooze. Push and ooze. Eleven silent, raw lumps stood to her right, ready for the oven. Only three more to go. She brushed aside a sweaty, escaped lock, smearing goo across her brow. Reaching for a cloth with the other hand, she stopped short seeing it also covered with the sticky paste.

Voices from the other room rolled in, rising and falling in response to His. Clearly absorbed in Him, they also eyed the kitchen, she knew, anticipating what only she could produce, desired to produce, must produce—for Him. She turned quickly back to kneading her gift, but caught sight of newly cut lamb ribs waiting for the grill. They, of course, needed stew to start first, which called for more water to boil the still unsliced onions. "This is impossible!" she despaired through gritted teeth.

Throwing down cloth she strode through doorway, stood before the seated man and, with sloppy hands jabbed into hips, towered over Him and demanded, "Lord, don't you care that my sister has left me to do the work by myself? Tell her to help me!"

So, what happened the last time your frustration drove you to rebuke the one you call Lord for not caring?

**Proverbs 19:3   Hebrews 2:5-18   Luke 10:38-42
1 Peter 5:5-7   John 10:1-18**

103. The Big Gun

The two pilots regarded the situation below. On the left, the pilot under instruction imagined himself descending to enter the canyon, following the river wedged between rocky cliffs, making the tight left turn up the mountain draw, and only then seeing the airstrip just moments before landing. He realized that as soon as he banked left, he would also commit them to touching the ground—someplace. Could he guarantee the runway? Trees and hard rock presented themselves as the sole alternatives.

He turned to the right and asked, "Brian, why don't you make this one? I haven't been here before, and I'd rather watch you the first time."

The instructor smiled and thought, "This guy is going to do all right. He recognized his limits and resisted pride's push beyond his abilities." Experienced hand claimed the throttle and wheel as he entered the practiced turn into the gorge.

In many of life's situations correct procedure says, "Call for help when in over your head." Wisdom counsels, "Seek advice when you can no longer handle it." So, no surprise when we view life as the sum of situations. After all, we deal successfully with little problems. And when tough spots stop us, we know to call in the Big Gun. After the rescue, we thank Him, promise to call again at the next insurmountable obstacle, and then resume our own navigation.

Unfortunately, we sometimes forget whose world it really is. True life centers not on us and our world, but rather on God and His world. He grants us an undeserved privilege by inviting us into His Kingdom.

So, what happened the last time you realized that you had actually been asking God to bless your plan rather than inquiring how He wanted you to participate in His?

**Psalm 24:1-2; 140:7-8   John 15:1-8   Proverbs 15:22
Hebrews 1:1-4   Luke 22:39-44**

104. The Big Party

A river grows—trickle to rivulet, rill to brook, stream to tributary. Ever moving, never stopping it carves its sinuous course from beginning mist to completed sea. Though it forms one body, start to finish, some see every bend as a separate place, every canyon a distinct world unconnected and unaffected.

o, too, our lives seem unique, independent, untouched by those who passed before—before the modern times, before we mastered space, marginalized nature, managed time, and manipulated life. "Old fashioned" insults, pinning us to a superseded past, too trivial, too naïve, too unsophisticated for relevance today.

We forget that life neither began nor ends with us. Instead, God placed us inside His larger story – one character within the flow of many. What our ancestors did before determines what we believe now. What we do today forms what our grandchildren's great-grandkids will believe tomorrow.

So, what happened the last time you realized that the party you heard was actually a great cloud of witnesses cheering you on?

**Matthew 22:29-33   1 Thessalonians 4:13-18   Acts 1:3-9
Hebrews 11:1-12:1**

105. Hanging On

White knuckles drove her nails deep, leaving furrows in the hope-chest lid.

"Marsha, we have to run—now!" her sister said through clenched teeth, heaving, arms wrapped around the girl's ankles. Smoke billowed into the room. Flames licked between far wall and ceiling.

"I won't leave it, I won't! It's all we have left of mom," she declared.

"That's … not … true," her sister spat, punctuating words with jerks on Marsha's legs. "She gave us you. You're worth lots more than old clothes and pictures!" Marsha screamed frustration and snapped open her grip just as sister yanked again. The two girls tumbled backwards out the bedroom door, across the small landing, and down the steep, narrow stairs. As they slammed into the wall at the bottom, the roof and ceiling collapsed into the upstairs room, showering them with bits of burning wallpaper and curtain. Clambering, crawling on all fours, they bolted through the front door, off the porch, and into a gasping heap on the lawn.

Consuming present challenges often signal us to remember past blessings. After all, what do we have that we haven't received from Him? What do we have that won't go back to Him?

And I'm curious. What happened the last time you realized that, during this in-between time we call life, all of it still belongs to Him?

Job 1:20   Psalm 77:1-11   Acts 7:48-50   1 Corinthians 4:6-7

106. Finding the Target

Chaos mixed the two armies into deadly melee. Organized tactics disappeared. Swords slashed unchosen targets. Spears pierced friend and foe alike. Daggers slashed from under-foot. Arrows rained. Death or deliverance came to just and unjust by chance, in moments too tangled to plan. "Luck," some said, clutching charm. "Fate," others declared, stroking amulet.

Some days, ordered life's basics overwhelm us. Too much, too fast, too hard tumbles us. Disappointment erodes the ground beneath. Our best efforts stumble and bumble through a speeding chain of days. We're on top only for the instant before the wave dashes us into the rocks again. Think? Manage? Meditate? Good ideas, yet the 'how' part eludes us, consistently visible and always out of reach.

But God found Israel's wicked king Ahab in a mad, fighting throng. Though hiding in disguise, a random shaft delivered prophesied judgment. Likewise, though lost amidst life's mayhem, promised favor pinpoints us precisely.

So, what happened the last time you realized that only the lunacy of the Lord's peace kept you near any definition of sanity?

2 Chronicles 18:28-34   Philippians 4:4-7   Matthew 6:3-4
1 Timothy 1:7   Luke 12:4-7

107. Coasting in the Good Times

Joseph sat back, stunned and frozen. Surely the rabbi's sad eyes spoke of someone else from another land or time. But like gangrene in a putrid wound, dark certainty raced through him, banishing peace, vanquishing joy, extinguishing light, destroying the dream. Mary. Pregnant. Their talks of sweet truth by the barley field—all lies? Her deep fountain eyes—cesspools? And who did it? He knew of others interested regardless of public pledges. Was he ever the real candidate? Or had she played him the fool to leverage another into hasty consummation? Wooden, like the timber he plied, Joseph arose and walked into the night heedless of path or time hoping only for bear or bandit or cliff to execute quick mercy.

While we coast in the good times, our old fears quietly regain power. Unnoticed, they lie in wait. Then, when life tests us beyond what we can control, overcome, endure, or even understand, they leap from ambush, destroy trust, and leave a smoking trail of doubt that cries, "Where's God in all this?"

Stretching always confronts us with impossible dilemmas, traps us behind insurmountable obstacles, and hurts like crazy. We call it trouble and survive only by clinging to Jesus. God calls it a gift to encourage growth. Coasting, on the other hand, always presents reasonable options, shows us attainable objectives, and feels just fine. We call it normal and work hard to perpetuate it. God calls it a gift for rest and healing. The problem, of course, comes when we mistake feeling good for His peace.

So, what happened the last time you realized how much harder it is to walk with God in the good times than in the bad?

**Matthew 1:18-25; 17:14-20   Ephesians 3:14-21   Luke 12:13-21
Revelation 3:14-22   John 9:39-41**

108. His Time

Stand in a field. Look left and right, forward and backward, up and down. Take a step or two or three. Strength enables horizontal movement. Airplanes allow ascents beyond a jump. Big shovels permit descents past the basement. We see where we want to go, and move as we choose.

But what about time? From present, we remember past, prohibited from any return to repair bad choices. From today we race to imagined future, denied any control of speed. Time cages all creation in a universal constant that yields to no force and responds to no appeal.

Why then, if God issues neither work-compactor nor time-brake, does He assign more tasks than allotted days will contain? In our darker, secret thoughts, we judge Him unfair. Doesn't He know how much we have to do?

Fortunately, time responds to trust just like money. We watch Him provide funds to feed kids, buy shoes, fuel airplanes, and send missionaries. But maybe we missed His stretching demo—the one where two widows' coins outweigh philanthropists' endowments. The truth is, He always sizes gifts of His time to meet the need.

So, what had you surrendered the last time you finished two day's work before Monday lunch?

**Joshua 10:1-15   1 Corinthians 10:13   2 Kings 20:8-11
Hebrews 13:20-21   Mark 12:41-44**

109. No Eraser

An inspirational email repeated a great mystery of Christian life: "The more precisely you plan, the harder destiny hits you."

The Bible says, "Plan, dummy. Even ants have sense to store up food for the winter." Unfortunately, it also teaches us the futility of counting on what we'll do a year from now in another city, when life five minutes in the future remains an invisible guess and mostly beyond our control.

So, what gives? Plan or just wait for life to happen? The answer lies in deep surrender, not to consultant or counselor, but to the Agenda Writer. The trick to that, of course, is in giving Him the pencil, and then throwing the eraser away.

So, what happened the last time you allowed Him to write on the tablet of your heart?

**Proverbs 6:6-11; 20:4; 24:27   John 5:19-21; 6:53-69
2 Corinthians 3:1-3**

110. Question of Trust

In mile-high flight above twisted jungle, we pilots trust that:
Fuel will ignite.
Electrons will flow and jump in the right places.
Wings and major pieces will remain attached.
Propellers will convert rotary motion into thrust.

Even unbelieving aviators trust that;
Air density, temperature, and mixture will persist as before.
Aerodynamic laws will continue without repeal.
Gravity will remain constant.
Earth's rotation will neither speed nor slow significantly.

If four wing-attach bolts merit trust thousands of feet above bog and branch, what trust limits apply to the bolt maker's Creator? After your honest heart affirms, "I trust You, Lord…"

what happens when He asks you:
What do you trust me for?
Who do you trust me with?
How far do you trust me?
How long do you trust me?

Job 38:1-41   Colossians 1:15-20   Luke 14:25-27
Hebrews 13:8   John 14:1

111. Navigating Life

Flowing mane a triumphant banner, flying tail a proud flag, the glistening steed races over hill and plain. Speed beyond the fast. Strength greater than the mighty. Horses' fluid motion fascinated cave painters, Bible writers, Mongols, Sioux, and moviegoers—each enraptured by powerful elegance, imagining a melding of character and spirit.

Melding, indeed. We often navigate through life like horses—mouth first, walking all over our food. We ask for daily bread then, with crumbs on still on chin, cry "Gimmee!" We ignore His gifts—food, abilities, love, and circumstances—lusting instead for our own distorted visions. Never satisfied, we call the present deficient. Never content, we forget that the same God igniting stars also grants every breath and heart beat.

So, what did He show you the last time you realized that you were treating His grace to you like an obligation due you?

**Deuteronomy 6:10:12   Colossians 2:16-19   Psalm 78:1-72
2 Peter 3:3-7; 4:3-4   1 Corinthians 4:7**

112. The Lone Tree

He ran hard, new sandals slapping sharp echoes in the deserted alley. Unfamiliar exertion sapped strength from his short, pudgy body. Breath came in raspy heaves. Feet pummeled cobblestone. Embroidered robes flew behind. Sweat oozed from under his turban, stinging his eyes. He knew who entered the city.

He veered right through a narrow gap between houses, burst onto the main road, and collided with two men. They turned but, seeing who lay there, checked oaths and glared distain instead. He jumped up, hands on knees, gasping, searching left and right. The thick throng spread all along the road.

He straightened. "Stand aside!" he commanded. The dense horde ignored him. He bounced on tiptoes. High backs and tall heads blocked passage and view. Cheers grew louder. Praises drew closer. Almost before him, yet hidden beyond convulsing mob, the retinue approached.

Then he saw a lone tree at road's edge to the right, still ahead of the pack. Fierce will arose from unknown depth. New energy flowed from untapped source. He ran faster than before, reached the trunk, and leapt into the lowest branches. Pull. Step. Pull. Step. Just in time. The entourage reached the tree and stopped below him. One face looked up, smiled, and beckoned, "Zacchaeus, come down immediately. I must stay at your house today."

So, I'm curious, the last time a crowd blocked your way to Jesus, where did you find a sycamore, and what did it look like?

**Deuteronomy 4:29-31   Luke 19:1-10   Proverbs 28:5
1 Peter 4:3-4   Isaiah 55:1-7**

113. Sure Knowledge

The packing juggernaut advances, relentlessly devouring office cubicles in methodical, discreet steps. Decorations gone. An hour later, no partition. Then, a desk empty, lamp cold and dark. Stuff leaves through gapping door. Friends don't reappear. A never admitted, child's niggling fear wonders, "Where does it all go? To a pit? To oblivion? Am I next?"

Faith, on the other hand, retorts, "Sweat not thyself. All appears on the other side, in the sunny land to the North." Faith, indeed. Our confidence rests on sure knowledge that Idaho exists and trust that burly chaps carrying boxes put them into trucks actually going there. We've seen both and believe both.

Jesus, on the other hand, challenges, "Because you have seen me, you have believed; blessed are those who have not seen and yet have believed." We happily accept the illogical, big-picture promise that we will move to heaven someday but sometimes stumble when broken planes strand us, or to-do's overrun us.

So, what happened the last time you rejected His grace just because you couldn't see it?

**Proverbs 16:9   Romans 1:18-20   John 14:1-4; 20:24-31
2 Corinthians 4:16-18**

114. Peak and Valley

Retreat sounds foul, hints cowardice, whispers weak will, and smears capitulation stink. We reward victors, laud champions, and extol winners. Epic tales scorn quitters, but honor overcomers. The Lord calls us "more than conquerors." Shouldn't we advance? Jesus warns that even looking back excludes us from the Kingdom. Shouldn't we attack? If battle talk compels us forward, why retreat for a weekend's contemplation?

The truth is, the same gain accrues to us that Israelites received, marching mute around a city. The same blessing drenches us that God's army obtained when soldiers followed singers into battle. The same banquet awaits us as our Commander earned when he lay on a cross and offered open palms to steel nails.

So, what happened the last time you gained victory's peak by way of surrender's dark canyon?

**Psalm 121:1-2   Matthew 5:1-10   Isaiah 40:27-31
John 12:23-26**

115. Hotter than the Sun

Lightning hits fast, hard, and five times hotter than the sun's surface. It strikes from cloud or clear sky when it wants and where it wants, destroying computers, bursting trees, and igniting conflagration. We awe at its beauty from afar, yet wisely cower and hide when close. Only fools stand tall in open, rainy fields. Most die when hit.

Sometimes our wild, unruly, Creator bursts upon us with neither invitation nor warning. Hot, uncontainable, and totally beyond our control, He appears when He wants, does what He chooses, and speaks to whomever He desires. We admire His majesty in stained glass or holy hymn, but it is, indeed, a fearful thing to fall into the hands of the living God. Who can stand in the day of His appearing?

Yet, some idiots climb to house peak in wet storm, raising hands, stretching higher, straining closer. What morons choose to play lightning rod? Only those tried, convicted, and condemned to certain death, knowing they live solely by massive infusions of grace. When struck, they explode, scattering wanton blessing that ignites holocausts of His favor.

Do you remember that fearful joy when He poured Himself through you, from His world into yours?

**Malachi 3:1-2   2 Corinthians 1:8-11   Mark 12:30
Hebrews 10:30-31   Romans 12:1**

116. Weakness in Strength

"Why delay?" Micah grumbled to the soldier waiting in the dark beside him. "If we strike them head-on as before, the uncircumcised dogs will flee as before." They peered at the distant fires of the Philistine camp—a horde invading a second time to dislodge the newly crowned monarch.

"But the king inquires of the Lord," his companion reasoned.

"What's to inquire?" Micah protested. "We know who to fight," he pointed with spear tip, "and we know how to fight." He grinned with raised sword. "No mystery befuddles us. The way ahead is clear. Why wait?

Troops behind stirred suddenly, opening a path in their midst. "We go around," David said as he reached them. "We wait among the myrtle trees for the Lord's sign then hit them from the rear."

"But David," Micah asked, forgetting fresh titles, "they lay straight ahead, overripe fruit for picking. Why the extra march and stealth?"

"I do not know, Micah. This battle looks to be an easier victory than last time. Nonetheless, we go the way the Lord commands."

When we despair, we weep before Him. When we fail, we ask His forgiveness. When we fall, we plead for His mercy. When perplexity overwhelms us, we seek Him. When disaster engulfs us, we run to His high tower.

But when we know the way, do we seek His direction? When we speak from experience, do we ask His counsel? When we work with practiced skill, do we implore His help? When we stride in right confidence, do we desire His strength? When we bask in victory, do we tremble before Him?

So, what happened the last time, in the middle of a really good day, you realized your desperate need for Jesus?

2 Samuel 5:17-25   Romans 4:1-8   Psalm 44:6-8
2 Corinthians 11:16-12:10

117. Rewind Button

"So, you wanna go back to Egypt ..." the song observes. But what's wrong with that? They need a witness there too, don't they?

Right ... History and prophets agree about slavery to the world rather than freedom in the Spirit. And serving earthly kings rather than the King of kings. Not to mention, worshiping hand-made idols in place of the Living God.

But Jesus—never content to leave well enough alone—probes deeper. We prefer old, He says, because we know it. We crave familiar because we predict its next move. We lust after worn paths leading to safe, comfortable dens but abhor incorrigible new ways. To our old nature, the alternative remains unthinkable.

Perhaps, that's why—out of creation's four expanded dimensions: three of space and one chronological—time is one-way. Flying to Boston and back presents little challenge. Changing speed or direction through history, however, defies us. God designed creation to continually confront us with a simple choice—hide from the uncontrollable unknown, or trust the uncontrollable God. Divine irony allows all to arrive regardless of choice. Some tumble in thrashing, kicking, and screaming. Others walk in smiling.

So, what happened the last time you realized just how glad you were that time doesn't have a rewind button?

**Exodus 14:10-12   Luke 9:62   Numbers 23:19
Philippians 3:12-14   Job 38:1-41**

118. Understood Truth

Aviation's collective wisdom declared tail-wheel aircraft superior to nose-wheel aircraft on rough airstrips. Makes sense. Bounding 3,000 pounds of aluminum at sixty mph over holes, rolls, and rocks imperils spindly nose-wheels. Hitting a bump wrong snaps it off. Tail-wheels, on the other hand, trail behind with no mass smashing them into mud and stone. They bounce and bob superficially, unneeded until taxi and park time. Beefy main wheels take the brunt of abuse as engineers designed.

But in the Amazon, we rescued a pilot every couple of months, stuck at a jungle airstrip with a flat tail-wheel tire, a broken tail-wheel assembly, a broken tail-wheel cable, or a broken tail-wheel mounting. Meanwhile, our nose-wheel aircraft took off and landed from the same strips every day for seventeen years with never a nose-wheel problem.

Did years of aeronautical experience accumulate wrong wisdom? Hardly. Rather, it stopped accepting challenges to set conclusions. Likewise, Pharisees, dedicated to speak truth against a secular onslaught, missed the very one their detailed education pointed to. Once convinced they understood truth's appearance, they ceased looking for anything else.

So, what happened the last time your assumptions rose up and bit you because you neglected to ask the right question?

**Proverbs 18:17   John 5:31-47   Mark 12:28-34
1 Timothy 3:14-16   Luke 8:16-18**

119. Mysterious Mash

The long walk with Jesus finally changed us. We started doing right things, perhaps because He said we're supposed to. Or maybe because He said bad things would happen if we didn't. Or possibly because He said He loved us. Or pragmatically because we saw His ways blessing others. And it all proved true. He corrected errors, but never let us down nor defaulted nor deserted. Our very desires changed from the inside out, seemingly by themselves. Eventually we found that we really wanted only to serve Him, please Him, glorify Him, do His will—whatever it was. That surrender brought settled, solid peace that made no human sense.

Unfortunately, tucked away in the folds of contentment, also tagged along the idea that we'd reached the safe haven at last. We had, after all, endured many hard fights. A little rest would be nice. Then unnoticed and certainly unbidden, worry began oozing up, muddying the clear stream we found in the high place. We'd sing that we'd give our all to Jesus, but sudden anxiety surprised us, tarnishing joy with nameless concerns and second thoughts.

When we asked, "What gives?" He exposed our divided heart. On one side, a genuine desire to do His will. On the other, fearful lust for our own significance. He warned us that the double-minded man was unstable in all he did and shouldn't expect anything from God. Fortunately, He also promised that "whoever wants to save his life will lose it, but whoever loses his life for me will find it."

So, the last time you realized your deepest desire was a mash of flesh and spirit, did you give up or move forward to attempt the impossible?

**Luke 12:16-21; 14:26   Philippians 4:6-7   Romans 12:3-8
James 4:7-10**

120. Mass Dictates

Saturn's largest ring looks solid through Earth-bound telescopes. For years educated imagination envisioned a billion pebbles circling the planet like dancers, waltzing in polite promenade. The Cassini spacecraft's visit, however, revealed a violent roller-derby instead.

Rather than occasional, demur touch of elbow splayed too wide, orbiting stones smash and crash continually. They form giant, hundred-foot clumps and then dash themselves to bits against fellow travelers moments later.

If farther from the mighty orb's gravity, they might coalesce into small moons; even farther from its dominion, one large moon. Saturn's mass, however, dictates otherwise. The giant sphere's influence spreads chaos and disunity.

So, what happened the last time you found yourself orbiting the wrong planet?

Exodus 23:2-3   1 Corinthians 15:33
Proverbs 13:20; 14:7; 26:4   2 Timothy 3:1-9   Romans 16:17-19

121. Sitting On Top

Uzziah strode up the great stairs. He pushed off each step with purpose and the measured pace of confidence. His bevy of attendants fluttered as he passed through the open doors.

"Your Majesty, is this wise?" a secretary warned.

"Nonsense!" the king assured him. "Am I not the Lord's anointed even as my forefather, David, wrote? Am I not giving honor and glory to God?"

"Well yes, but ...

Uzziah ignored the pleading minion and picked up a golden censer. He fumbled with the unfamiliar latch, opened the cover, then searched for the tongs. Spotting them to the left, he switched the censer to his right hand, lifted the tongs from their peg and reached for the glowing coals.

"Stop!" a command bellowed from behind.

Uzziah whirled about to find Azariah and 80 other priests rushing into the temple to confront him   .

Eventually we understand that when we exhaust our energy, run out of ideas, have no other recourse, and, overwhelmed by superior force, come to the point of final defeat, Jesus steps in and shows Himself strong through our weakness. Even death itself is not immune to His intervention.

But what about when all goes well? When vibrant health flows through our veins? When wise counsel and insight rolls off our lips? When prudent planning and sound discipline offer an abundant harvest? When we sit atop our game and success's justly earned rewards accumulate about our feet? Does weakness find a welcome?

Depends on which weakness we see – that bred of fear, or what flows from honor. The required weakness contains no cowardice, gullibility, impotence, or mental deficiency. Instead He looks for a freewill offering of all the strengths, abilities, and gifts already bestowed upon us. The weakness He seeks makes us neither fearful sops nor lousy lovers. Instead, we become brother in arms with the King of kings.

So, what happened the last time, when at the peak of your form, He showed you how desperately you needed Him?

Exodus 15:2   Daniel 4:30-34   Judges 6:11-16
Ephesians 1:3-5   2 Chronicles 26:16-20

122. Two Gray Beards

Two gray beards talk in hall,
Two gray beards lean on wall.
Two gray beards still with life,
Two gray beards still with fight.

Two gray beards speak not of when,
Two gray beards were younger men.
Two gray beards plan instead,
Two gray beards look ahead.

Two gray beards with open eyes,
Two gray beards reach for prize.
Two gray beards work on earthly shore,
Two gray beards go out once more.

Two gray beards joined to Source,
Two gray beards know the course.
Two gray beards made of clay,
Two gray beards point the way.

So, what happened the last time God astounded you with an Abraham? Or, made you one?

**Psalm 37:25; 71:1-24   2 Corinthians 4:5-7   Jeremiah 18:1-6
Philippians 3:12-14   1 Corinthians 13:11-12**

123. Strong Focus

The pilot stepped over a gas hose snaked across the temporary ramp and stopped. Half the cargo for his flight lay in a heap. "Where's Pancho? This does not help my day at all," he said to no one. He sighed, stooped, and wrestled luggage and 100-pound rice bags into the cargo pod. Finished, he buckled his lone passenger into the copilot seat. Then, still sweating, he strapped himself into place.

Carefully, he moved through the checklist, deliberately speaking each task aloud. Finally, engine running, helmet on, and gages good, he eased off the brakes. With gentle touch, he added power and looked to the left. The unfamiliar path to the runway was evident enough. He visualized where he'd angle further left to pass through the gate out of their borrowed quarters. "Just have to stay in the middle," he cautioned himself. "Still time to …"

Frantic pounding on his right shoulder jerked him around to his wide-eyed passenger gasping, "Capitán …" The windshield filled with parked airplane and wide-mouthed Pancho on a fueling ladder. He stabbed brakes hard, halting the spinning propeller five feet from collision.

Sometimes, strong focus on where we want to go blinds us to where we are going. So, what happened the last time you found yourself so intent on a plan that reality's snapping teeth snuck up and jumped out of the bushes in front of you?

**Joshua 9:1-21   1 Corinthians 10:11-12   Proverbs 14:12; 15:22
1 Peter 5:8   Acts 27:1-44**

124. Working with Turkeys

The Zapotecs ruled a large swath of southern Mexico from the Oaxaca Valley. During their 700-year peak they quarried huge stone blocks without metal tools, moved the multi-thousand pound pieces miles from the source, and then raised them into expansive palaces, using human muscle-power alone. Their astronomers discovered the 365-day year, and their nobles developed a complex civil-service bureaucracy. But these intelligent folks also ate enemy captives, convicted criminals, and adulteresses at public ceremonies.

Eventually their kingdom devolved into competing chiefdoms until swallowed by the Aztecs. However, their legacy lives on. Modern Zapotec villages, five miles apart on good road, speak mutually unintelligible languages, frequently fight land wars, and cooperate on almost nothing. We believers, of course, shake our heads in bemused dismay. We cluck about cooperation, extol mutual respect's value, and point wisely at Jesus' love teaching.

Love, indeed. We read that Jesus declares love above all. We agree love glues the Church. We understand mutual love trumps all testimony. Yet, a joke exposes embarrassing truth: "How can I fly like an eagle when I have to work with a bunch of turkeys?" We laugh aloud, but resonate secretly. Loving neighbors proves difficult because they, like us, look horrible and smell badly. Yet in this hopeless situation God works a great miracle. He advances His Kingdom through us because He knows the secret—don't look at the mess, see the jewel.

So, what happened the last time you found gold in the trash pile?

Matthew 9:9-13   1 Corinthians 1:10-31; 13:1-13
Luke 19:1-10   2 Corinthians 5:16-21

125. Triumphant Entry

Clop, clop, clop, clop, the little donkey's pace steadied. Shaky at first, young hooves beat cadence on stony street. Head down, he leaned forward into unaccustomed burden. He'd seen mama carry sacks, beams, and bales and wondered if he could too. Now, he knew.

Clop, clop, clop, clop, cloths over his back danced in rhythm with each step more sure than last. The load shifted slightly, and he almost stopped. But it remained in place, so he kept going, climbing towards the gate, confidence growing, strong muscles showing.

Clop, clop, clop, clop, his head bobbed higher. Men walked along either side, a few at first, then more lined the sides, arms high, mouths open, noisy voices swelling. Branches sprang up. Some waved. Some fell on the path before him, gifts from those he pleased.

Clop, clop, clop, clop, he danced amid cheers, tears, and song. The throng pressed close, but the way forward kept open just enough. He pushed harder up the last rise and then through the arch. Din rose to roar as he triumphantly entered Jerusalem.

So, what happened the last time you realized that all the excitement and praise was not for you, but the One you carried?

**Zechariah 9:9   2 Corinthians 4:1-18   Matthew 21:1-11
Galatians 2:20**

126. Alternate Reality

A wise woman once said "Holiness is having nothing to hide."
"Certainly!" we intone, "I don't smoke, drink, or chew nor run with those that do.
Saved while young, raised in church, I keep the Golden Rule.
Faithful to spouse, good to kids, I teach Sunday school."
A great song, indeed. But what about our other life, the secret one? What about the alternate reality we hide in heart and stroke in thought?

For men: 'romp in fantasy' thoughts. For women: 'lost in romance' thoughts. For all of us, the fearful thoughts, the powerful thoughts, the greedy, jealous, worried, deceptive thoughts rehearsed, nurtured, and lived inside where no one sees or knows. Never acknowledged, invisible, yet vivid, our private planet's lurid power generates emotions greater than real life and bonds stronger than true love.

God speaks no pointless words when He warns of idols and other gods, of wealth's allure, stolen glance's seduction, and control's intoxication. He shares no frivolous jokes when He rails against shining white sepulchers concealing corruption. He knows our frame and that the stronger our painted walls, the longer the festering toxin brews within, poisoning heart, mind, and soul.

Fortunately, He offers to break down every dividing wall, making one new man, one complete woman. He entreats us to open every door when He knocks. Surrender our secret world. Trade muffled, hidden lies for shouted, public truth. Crawl from under shame. Climb atop the Rock. Don't give up. Don't despair. The Peacemaker heals inner wars one battle at a time.

So, what did you learn the last time He cured your doubled thoughts?

**Matthew 23:27-28 James 4:7-10 2 Corinthians 10:5
Revelation 3:14-22 Ephesians 2:14-18**

127. Impossible Reality

Throw a ball at a wall. Will it pass through leaving both unscathed? Unlikely, though your family pitches every minute for a thousand generations. But quantum mechanics reveals that sub-atomic particles leave no hole when they penetrate barriers they shouldn't. They also arrive before they leave and occupy multiple locations at once—for starters.

Common sense says, "Impossible!" Yet the computer on our desk and the hospital's MRI depend on these ridiculous truths. Comprehensible or not, we gladly accept their absurd fruit.

Likewise, we Jesus followers claim intimate familiarity with preposterous truth. We know that one suffered punishment for all. We agree that a lamb is a lion. We teach that the last shall be first. We proclaim the dead will surely live again.

Why then, if such absurdities pose no threat, do we revert to Christian life based on law? What compels us to measure progress along His impossible way by our possible deeds?

And what happened the last time the fog cleared suddenly and you grabbed the controls in fright because you found yourself cruising the highway of grace?

**Luke 13:30   Galatians 3:1-4   2 Corinthians 5:14-15
1 Thessalonians 4:15-16**

128. Taking it Back?

We dedicate babies to God, set apart airplanes for His service, and consecrate buildings to His glory. But why commit tangible valuables to invisible ideals? What anticipation compels our promises? We set china up carefully in glass cabinets for all to see. Are other treasures so hidden that God needs help finding them? Does the common background so obscure us that only unique ceremonies attract divine attention? What, exactly, do we expect Him to do?

Certainly, beneath form and custom, we harbor feelings ranging from hope to conviction that He does, in fact, intervene in the affairs of men. But the truth is, dedication neither tricks a wily deity nor woos a reluctant creator. Instead, dedication capitalizes on a great mystery —our own words reveal our heart's darkness, but they also carry His power, reflect His light, and accomplish His will.

Dedication gives us opportunity to declare intent we can't complete, choose ends we can't reach, and trust for righteousness we can't attain. Ceremony's words only begin the transformation of symbolic into real. The difficult test, of course, comes in the long-term, daily surrender to the Spirit we invoked at the start.

So, the last time you placed your heart's desire into His hands, what happened when you realized you were about to jerk it back?

**Isaiah 64:6   Mark 10:27   Matthew 5:33-37; 10:22;
Luke 9:23; 15:16-20**

129. Power's Perception

Evening sun glared off the sea below Mt Carmel, lighting rock, trees, and men in stark red and shadow relief. Four hundred fifty Baal prophets lay panting on dusty ground. Bloody from a myriad ceremonial cuts, they lacked strength even to brush away flies engulfing them and the rotting meat atop their still un-kindled offering.

The crowd faced Elijah instead. The wood and freshly slaughtered meat of his stone altar dripped from his ordered drenching. "How long will you waver between two opinions?" he challenged. "Choose who you will serve —Baal or the Lord!" He turned to the altar, raised his arms and called to God. A blinding column of flame smashed down from the sky consuming meat, wood, rock, soil, and water.

The people froze an instant then fell to faces crying, "The Lord— He is God! The Lord—He is God!" Revival swept throng and countryside alike. Yet, within a few years these same people bowed to Baal again.

The truth is, overwhelming power commands great obedience only while power's perception persists. Remove force from human nature, and chaos fills the welcoming vacuum. Love, on the other hand, never, ever fails. It sustains beyond endurance, fills the bottomless gap and goes the unreachable distance.

So, what happened the last time you realized that God spoke no metaphor when He called Himself Love?

**1 Kings 18:1-46   2 Peter 2:10-12   1 Corinthians 13:1-13
1 John 4:13-16**

130. Now It Was Worse

Moses trembled face down on the ground, arms outstretched. Short gasps inhaled dust, but sweaty palms turned dirt to mud. Outside his tent, the mob swelled, grew louder, bolder. A few men provided a shallow barrier, but that wouldn't last. There were too many, too desperate, too angry. And he'd seen stones in hands, hefted, tested, ready.

For three months God led them from place to place. He met every need, every day. But still they cried, "Moses, give us water to drink! Are you trying to kill us, and our kids and animals?"

Now it was worse. The answer to his plea was neither rain, nor unseen river, nor even escape. Instead, God told him to take his staff, go before the people and strike the rock at Horeb. Sure, God could bring water from stone. But what chance did a man have to reach it alive? He imagined the first hit cracking bone, the second, the third…

He clenched both fists, nails gouging sand, knuckles white. One more breath, deep, perhaps the last one free, then he rose, pushed open the flap, and strode out to a thousand furious faces.

Sometimes, just like dying to live, slapping fear's face opens the shortest path to victory. So, what happened the last time you came out of hiding and attacked bedeviling dread?

**Exodus 17:1-7   Isaiah 35:3-4; 41:10   Psalm 27:1-3
2 Corinthians 7:5-7**

131. So Slight

Marian pulled her cloak tighter and pressed into the cold wind. Bending low, head down, she picked her way up the valley. Dull, low clouds still engulfed the hills ahead. She looked up hoping to see the right one, but spits of stinging rain forced her gaze back to her feet. All the bases looked alike, but the stories said only the tallest held the refuge. How would she know?

She reached them the next morning. Yet, within the draws and ravines, one hill seemed the same as any other. For many days she climbed hoping and descended disappointed. Hill after hill yielded only vacant tops, some surrounded by higher humps and others with short pleasant views. Maybe the stories were just stories as so many said—wishful thinking to comfort frightened children and cowardly adults.

Then one day she quit. "I give up!" she screamed at the sky and flopped to the ground devoid of strength even to despair. That's when she noticed it. So slight, she would've missed it standing. Something had pressed grass down into the dirt. And there, an arm's length away, another mark. And another. And another. In a line, they made a string winding up a low rise she would've rejected as too slight for the start of a proper hill.

So, what happened the last time the path up His holy mountain appeared only after you came to the end of yourself?

Isaiah 61:1-3   Luke 11:9   Psalm 23:1-3   2 Corinthians 4:7-11

132. Going in Circles

Straight-line thinking works great for construction projects, compound interest, fleeing burning buildings, and aerial navigation. Calculate the heading to your destination. If nothing tall and hard blocks the way, mark one straight line on the map. Measure the distance. Divide that by your speed to determine how long the trip takes. Calculate the fuel needed. If the plane will carry all the gas plus you, your lunch, your passengers and their cargo, you're good to go. After that, point the aircraft, and wait for the destination to appear.

Linear logic works so well, so often, we believe it ought to work for everything important. Makes sense, really. Find Jesus. Learn His Word. Join His Church. Serve His people. Arrive in Heaven. Short. Simple. Direct. Clear. No messing around. If so, why, despite our best efforts to the contrary, do we cower before old fears overcome, wrestle anew old doubts dispelled, and fight again old battles won? Does entropy erode His Kingdom like it rots creation? Does His strength wear out? Does His victory dissolve?

The truth is, He warned us, "I have much more to say to you, more than you can now bear." Like onion skins, His mercy peels us back thin layer by layer, circling, revisiting old lessons learned, cutting deeper, resting, and then returning to probe the limits again, pruning for growth rather than piercing, drawing out rather than judging sin's depth.

So, what happened the last time you looked at strangely familiar circumstances and realized that you'd been lost there before?

John 16:12-13   James 1:2-8   Hebrews 5:11-6:3

133. It's Here

Look outside the cockpit. We call that long line dividing Earth from sky, 'horizon'. Put the nose a bit below it to fly level. Raise it to climb. Lower it to descend. Align the wings parallel with the horizon to fly straight. Tip them right or left to turn. Safe flight depends on seeing what's really there.

What if clouds hide everything? No problem. The artificial horizon faithfully reports reality. "The horizon is here," it states. "Your left wing is low," it says. "Your nose is high," it observes. When we trust the instrument's revelation of truth, we fly secure.

But never mix visual and instrument flight. A ridge seen through mist mimics the horizon saying, "It's here," while the instrument says, "It's over there." Not knowing which to trust, we follow neither and find disaster instead.

Likewise, critiquing grace with law cripples. Judging faith by knowledge kills. So, what happened the last time you tried to manage your walk rather than follow the Lord?

**Psalm 26:2-3   Romans 8:1-17   Proverbs 3:19-26
2 Corinthians 3:4-6   John 15:5**

134. Heart Habits

We flew all week, peering through rain-spotted windshields as we scudded around low, drizzly ceilings. At the conference site every landing, each turn to taxi, churned the strip into a muddy bog. Furrows crisscrossed in a spider web maze, glistening silver in the rare, brighter gray. We slipped, slid, and sloshed about the plaza and runway, concentrating hard to avoid sinking into the softer spots or falling off the edge of the prepared areas. Takeoffs, though, presented little problem. We calculated the extra distance required to overcome mud's resistance and poured on 310 roaring, turbo-charged horsepower. The rudder took over directional control from the nose wheel, and the soft channel walls yielded easily to 3,000 plus pounds of charging aluminum. Like swamp boats, our huge tires quickly climbed atop the mire, floated, then flew. We finished the mission dirty and wet, but content.

The morning after the last departure, welcome sun returned with bright sky and brisk breeze, drying soaked airplanes, people, and villages. A few days later, one of our pilots drew the assignment to return to the conference site. Heavy with tanks of extra fuel to replenish our depleted remote cache, he touched down in the familiar spot and lowered the nose. The main wheels, set solidly into concrete-hard ruts, wrenched the plane left and, despite heavy braking, led it off the runway and down the short bank, where it stopped with nose in the creek and broken landing gear entangled in fallen logs.

Heart habits wear deep grooves into soul, ignoring both good intention and promise, pushing us face-first back into the cesspool. "Sorry," alone, lacks power and folds at the second or third temptation. God's Spirit, on the other hand, floats then lifts us above the steel tracks of doom. The irony, of course, is that the same heart that cuts the furrows is the only one that can request the power. As a pastor recently said, "We change our mind so that God can change our heart so that, together, we can change our way."

So, what happened the last time that you, like Saul promising to never chase David again, found yourself running the familiar path towards the swamp you thought you'd escaped?

**1 Samuel 26:17-21   Romans 7:21-25   Psalm 130:1-7
1 John 1:8**

135. One Leper Part 1

Suddenly, Micah hurt. Road pebbles dug into his knees. Pain! Could it be? He thrust out both hands from under ragged robe and splayed fingers wide. Ten good fingers again! He looked up. The healer standing over him grinned. Then, the grin grew serious, and the healer drew Micah to his feet.

He warned Micah sternly, "Don't tell anyone, but go, show yourself to the priest and offer the sacrifices that Moses commanded for your cleansing, as a testimony to them." Then he turned and, with his companions, continued down the road away from the village.

Two village men trailing the healer ran to Micah. "What did that man do to you?" they demanded. Micah drew back. He was unclean … or used to be … The men peered into his face, now with complete nose and smooth skin. A mother with son in tow inched nearer.

"Show us your hands," they insisted. He raised a complete set of new digits before astonished gapes.

The squirming boy broke free and ran to the village crying over and over, "The beggar has all his fingers and toes!"

Huddle grew quickly to crowd. They wanted to see him, wanted to hear him, wanted to touch him. Enfolding him, they drew him, Micah the outcast leper, inside their town and into their homes. The healer, on the other hand, could no longer enter a town. Popularity's sudden surge forced him to remain outside in lonely, remote places.

So, what happened when you realized that Jesus didn't swoop down from the sky to carry you away to safety but, instead, traded places with you?

**Mark 1:40-45   Hebrews 10:8-10   John 14:15   1 Peter 2:9-10
2 Corinthians 5:21**

136. One Leper Part 2

The crowd pressed tightly against the doorway. Micah's host, however, held them at bay, allowing only a few to enter at a time. They sat on the floor around his stool, eyes bright and eager. "Tell us," they begged. "What did he do?"

Micah repeated the story with little embellishment. The truth, after all, astounded everyone. "Yes, the Healer touched me," he confirmed. "No, He didn't heal me then; it was after he spoke. He commanded the leprosy to leave, and it did."

"Tell my sister!" a woman said. "And my uncle," her husband added. "They both live in Tecoa."

"Yes, we journey there tomorrow," Micah said exchanging mutual nods with his host. In the week since his cleansing, both curious and hopeful besieged him. But with Amaziah's help, he managed the mobs – and their donations. Real clothes wore better than grease rags. Real food tasted better than beggar's scraps. Real bed slept better than dirt cave. Real friends listened better than deformed wretches. And besides, after he recounted the tale, audiences set out en masse to find the Healer. They, too, needed God's miracles.

Eventually he'd have to get to Jerusalem and show himself to the priests. In the meantime, duty to spread marvelous news called. Just one more group to bless tonight, then he'd sleep until his predawn departure.

So, what happened the last time you hid disobedience with good ministry?

**1 Samuel 15 1-34   Luke 11:33-36   Matthew 23:23-28
Acts 5:1-11**

137. Beating Against the Wind

Stiff wind blew across the lonely, open place. A bird with stout heart crossed toward beckoning tree. Flap, flap, flap, flap, he beat against the wind, never advancing an inch. He slacked just a bit and drifted backwards. Renewing resolve, he beat harder and held position. Flap, flap, flap, flap, he beat against the wind at a twelve-foot height. Suddenly he dove, stroking down faster, leveling just above the grass, moving ahead a yard. Flap, flap, flap, flap, he beat against the wind at a one-foot height, never advancing an inch. Then, he rocketed up returning to twelve feet, losing a yard. Flap, flap, flap, flap, he beat against the wind, never gaining an inch. Dive; fly low. Climb; fly high. Never gaining an inch.

We set goals and pursue visions, striving against odds and opposition. The distant tree beckons, but invisible wind hinders. Flap, flap, flap, flap, we beat against the wind, never gaining an inch. Frustrated, we would even consider flying the other way—if only our tree lay downwind. What hidden hand holds us back? "Must be the World!" we declare. "The enemy fights against me!" we proclaim. "My own nature holds me back," we confess. "This is the Lord's testing, I must stay strong," we reason. Maybe. Maybe not. What if, in our flight towards the tree the Lord planted, we discover that it's the Holy Spirit blowing hard against us? Doesn't make sense. After all, we've grown beyond calling pleasure, power, or wealth, divine ends. And we understand laying aside life to glorify Him. So, why would He oppose us?

The truth is, like Abraham in his long wait for Isaac, we can hold cherished promise as a right due us. We forget that the Lord Himself, not His promise, is our inheritance. He defines who we are, not the role He assigns. Sometimes, His fierce love rescues by driving us away from our idol—the perverted godly goal.

So, what did you learn the last time you confused gift and Giver?

Ecclesiastes 8:16-9:1   Ephesians 2:14   Acts 17:24-34
Hebrews 12:1-12   Romans 1:18-25

138. Too Busy

Here I am again. Seems like way too long since we talked. Don't know why I wait until I'm ready to pop. Can't remember the last time I did only one thing at a time. Always have to multi-task just to keep up. Of course, that's the problem. I'm not keeping up. I work harder, and my list grows longer. I work longer and get less done.

I have wanted to talk, really. But something always comes up. Something with a deadline. Something urgent to someone, somewhere. I did have regular spots for You. Even put them into my calendar. But those somethings keep washing You right off the schedule.

Now, I'm so covered over that my agenda drowned, and I'm barely treading water. Any little ripple will send me with it, straight to the bottom. I'd like to stay and tell You more, but I've got to finish this report before the meeting and then do another flight. I'll get back to You when I have just a little more time.

So, what happened the last time you realized that if you're too busy to pray, you're too busy?

**Deuteronomy 6:4-12   Matthew 11:28-30   1 Kings 19:11-13
Philippians 4:10-13   Psalm 37:4-6**

139. Crucial Marathon

She ran fast, sent by command, focused on given purpose. Neither old nor young, she was slight but not fragile. White dress flowing, streaked, but whole. Long hair streaming, wild but untangled. Sweat glistened from determination, not exhaustion. Her feet beat a steady rhythm against stone, dirt, and thorny weeds. Her long legs pumped to the beat, pushing up and down, propelling her from rock to crag as she ascended the ridge. Along the spine she found open ground again and picked up speed. Exhale over four steps, then inhale. Out for four, then in. Steady, hard breathing for hard running, her steps kept time for this course's song. All her trips had a song, each one different, but each one sung. Hour after hour, dark or light, heat and rain, she ran on never slowing.

Then she came to the brow of a low cliff and stopped. Looking down into a festering swamp, she found the broad warrior gleaming black and gold. He stood legs apart over someone laying in the muck, too befouled to reveal name or age. Slowly, with neither hate nor pride, the mighty one raised his long sword high in the dank light. Weak eyes looked up, widening white against black slime. The strong arm above tightened, drawing back. Below, a gasping ripple popped up a hand in futile defense. Seeing her signal at last, she leapt over the edge, pounded hard down the hill, and dove atop the quivering creature. She turned to face the falling blade that stopped suddenly an inch from her throat.

Judgment gazed only a moment then nodded obedience. Sheathing his sword, he stepped back. Mercy stood, grasped the hand she'd laid atop, and drew me out of the putrid mess.

So, what happened the last time Jesus sent Grace racing to your rescue?

**Psalm 18:18-19; 23:6   Hebrews 4:14-16   Luke 5:32
James 2:12-13**

140. Info Wash

Chaos ruled the Roman Empire's rotting bones for a thousand years. Anarchy's waves devastated home, hearth, and harmony. Order and reverence perished. Curiosity and inspiration expired. Fire and sword obliterated everything.

Almost everything, that is. Turns out that light had friends after all. Irish believers built monasteries all across Europe. Alone they stood, isolated, defying the overwhelming terror tide. They kept history's memory, added to scientific understanding, and preserved scripture. Those candles guarded knowledge before hurricanes.

Today, knowledge washes over us—plentiful, but undervalued. We forget the bastions of knowledge, anchored in rock to turn back the dark. We forget that: God makes promises. God keeps promises. God is good. God gives good gifts. God gave Christ. Christ loves us. Christ saves us. Christ forgives us. Christ lives in us. Christ calls us. Christ leads us. Christ equips us. Christ sustains us. Christ heals us. Christ feeds us. Christ hears us. Christ answers us. Christ plans eternity. Christ plans our lives. Christ knows us. Christ desires us …

So, what happened the last time you discovered that, like bald Samson confronting swarming Philistines, you didn't know what you didn't know?

**Judges 16:18-21   Romans 10:1-4   Psalm 91:1-16; 139:1-12
Ephesians 1:3-14**

141. What Kind of Name

What kind of name is it that:
Entrusts itself freely to those least able to bear it with honor?
Risks everything on those demonstrated most unreliable?
Inspires nations, and then offers itself freely to brigands?
Breathes life into dust, and then grants rebels free use?
Adopts its abusers into its own family?
Forgives its executioners?
Embraces its perverters?
Saves its blasphemers?

It's the only name that:
Sits high above every other name that's named.
Speaks into existence everything from nothing.
Contains love enough to push out every fear.
Possesses all authority in heaven and earth.
Rewards those who hope in it.
Educates those who fear it.
Redeems those who call it.
Overcomes all obstacles—even defeat, disgrace, and death.

So, what happened that last time you saw what's written on your own forehead?

**Isaiah 53:1-12   1 John 4:4   Philippians 2:5-11
Revelation 14:1**

142. Going Nowhere Fast

The visitor shook her head, half worried and half amazed. How did people live in a jungle with heat, bugs, and isolation enough to drive anyone mad? The pilot, seeing her furrowed brow, tried to lighten the moment. "Well, this isn't the end of the world," he said grinning. As she snorted, he added, "But you can see the edge from here." She chuckled with him and climbed into the plane. He buckled her harness, gave the safety briefing, and settled into the command seat.

Sometimes jokes just band-aid fear, he mused. He spent his days like a frenzied demigod, hurtling his gleaming aluminum chariot skyward, speeding over a vast convoluted sea of green desolation. But speeding where? And who saw, anyway? God, sure. But did anyone with skin on really care? Was he wasting his life here, going nowhere fast? Edge of the world, indeed.

What do we call the boundary at the end of somewhere? Cutting edge or start of nowhere? Depends entirely upon what we plan to cut. Our ideal "somewhere" offers resource control (money), people control (power), intimacy control (relationship/sex), image control (significance), and status control (identity).

God's mysterious geography, on the other hand, defines "somewhere" not as a place, but as grace in action—bringing good news to the poor, binding up the brokenhearted, proclaiming freedom to the captive, comforting mourners, replacing ashes with beauty, mourning with gladness, and despairing with praise. Then, to mark the especially important nowheres, He plants righteous oaks.

So, what happened the last time, when lost on the backside of nowhere and stuck in the "slough of despond," you realized you were actually an acorn, planted by a stream?

Psalm 1:1-6   Matthew 25:1-46   Isaiah 61:1-11

143. Implement That Victory

The movie *Independence Day* tells the story of alien scavengers scourging the planet and obliterating the human race. People fight to save Earth, but the enemy's machines remain invincible behind an impenetrable shield. Then, the good guys manage to get aboard the alien's command ship and destroy it. This removes the protection around the smaller ships, and our heroes save the day.

Satan and his minions tried to obliterate the human race. People fought, but the enemy remained invincible for centuries. Fortunately, Christ came to Earth, defeated Satan, and removed the impenetrable shield. He then commanded His Body to implement that victory on Earth.

So, how is He granting those around you independence from darkness, despair, and death?

Isaiah 25:4-9   Romans 10:14-15   John 8:12
1 Corinthians 15:50-58

144. Armed and Dangerous

God's Kingdom advances inexorably, step-by-step, surely moving to achieve His ends. Strangely, He's delegated His plan to people—all very different, all very flawed, and all armed dangerously with free will. How can He possibly administer His grace through us? That it works at all has to be one of the greatest miracles ever. We'll understand only when we're with Him.

For now, though, from our finite, space-time perspective, we judge that a chief ingredient has to be a surrendered, willing heart.

How do the desires and passions He's placed in your heart work out as you minister today?

**Psalm 34:18; 51:17   1 Corinthians 1:26-31   Matthew 5:1-16
1 Peter 4:10-11**

145. Balancing the Ends

The last few mornings rose slowly, gray with low ceilings, damp and cold. Difficult flying perhaps, but stolen moments with hot mug in hand draw inner heart-questions out. "What does it all mean?" Of course, they counterpoint the hot, bright days to come. Days to fly far, fly fast, fly late. Days when all things seem possible. Days when meaning yields to doing.

Life in Christ demands balancing similar extremes. Where, in between the ends, do we walk?

The only sure guide is the Holy Spirit. He speaks to us in every area of life—our personal integrity, how we relate to people around us, how we plan an approach so that we don't slide off the end of a jungle airstrip.

Learning to hear Him accurately requires practice. Without that practice, we have little hope of administering His grace. Of course, administering that grace is how we practice. It's often called ministry.

So, how is He ministering through you these days?

**Isaiah 30:19-22   2 Timothy 2:15   John 14:25-27   1 Peter 4:10
Romans 12:9-21**

146. Super Bowl

Sometimes, when it was just me and the airplane suspended above a vast jungle, I felt the lonely stranger in a strange land. Those of us that fly rarely see each other. We're scattered all over the planet. Hidden in jungles. Isolated on the backside of deserts. Obscured in trackless mountains. Swallowed by city mobs.

But the Lord reminded me that we're members of the same family, parts of the same Body, citizens of the same Kingdom. He assured me that we don't run this race alone and unknown. As proof, He pointed to the huge crowds of enthusiastic fans leaning over the edge of the Celestial Coliseum, wearing funny hats, shouting, jumping, waving wildly, and cheering us on as we press towards the goal.

So, what happened the last time you heard the roar of the crowd while laboring alone?

Matthew 6:1-4   Ephesians 1:5; 2:19-22
1 Corinthians 12:12-13   Hebrews 12:1-3

147. Invisible Contrast

We swam with the human tides at the Oshkosh air show. We inhaled aviation, smelled engine oil, felt cold aluminum, and gawked at newly birthed aircraft. Anyone with an idea can design and market a service, a product, or even an airplane.

After so many years overseas, the free expression of creativity amazes and almost overwhelms. Nothing makes me appreciate living in America more than not living in America. And nothing makes me appreciate Kingdom citizenship more than listening to aliens. The rich contrast between light and dark before us every day is invisible to them.

Of course, healing the blind is a privilege of mission work. How is He opening the eyes of their hearts around you?

Isaiah 9:2   Acts 5:12-16; 26:16-18   Luke 11:33-36
Ephesians 1:18

148. Oranges in the Air

All managers are too busy. That's the nature of management—keeping the maximum number of oranges in the air without letting any hit the ground. The trick, when we're squinting into the sun, is to know which of the falling black dots are watermelons.

Fortunately, the Holy Spirit gives us discernment. He speeds our reactions to catch the big ones before they make a horrible mess and gives us peace to ignore those that are still a long way up there.

So, how has He helped you avoid major disaster lately?

**1 Kings 3:7-9   Hebrews 4:12-13   Ecclesiastes 8:2-6
James 1:2-8   Luke 11:11-13**

149. Strong Compulsion

Passion—maybe you feel it. Certainly you live it. It defies reason but submits to the heart. It comes from a simple desire to know God that suddenly explodes into an obsession to serve Christ. His will fuses with your desire so powerfully that you can't not do it.

You leave hearth and home for a strange place, inhabited by even stranger people. You don't know them, but Jesus does—intimately. He cares so much for them that He sends just the right tool to meet their needs.

So, O' passionate servant, what has He filled you with that is deeper than feelings? Tell me, what compels you so strongly that, even when you're fed up with problems, discouraged by disappointments, and have no energy to care anymore, you rise up and do it all again.

Ruth 1:1-4:22   2 Corinthians 3:1-3; 5:11-21   Jeremiah 20:9

About the Author

"I rarely experienced fear while flying. But my strongest memory, while hanging by one propeller and four wing attach-bolts over that vast jungle, was that Jesus was always very, very close. That's where my running conversation with Him grew from trickle to torrent."

Former MAF jungle pilot, Jim Manley, swims in a continual downpour of blessing and favor. His compilation of columns inviting contributions to the MAF newsletter, Around the World, will inspire you to see your life as an adventure, as well. Explore over a hundred examples of the Lord revealing Himself in life situations that change the Bible from printed page to living water.

Jim started following Jesus after a chance encounter while hitchhiking. A few years later he had secured an ideal middle class life—wife and children, a house in a mountain town, aviation business and a vibrant church. Life was good, life was understood. But he felt called to the ministry—not as a preacher or evangelist, but as a pilot. Mission Aviation Fellowship (MAF) sent Jim and family to Ecuador, South America. For 17 years he supported the work of several mission, translation, and humanitarian organizations. During his final six years there he also served as MAF's Ecuador program manager

After transferring to MAF's home staff in the USA he wrote print and web copy along with technical manuals. He served as editor for MAF's in-house newsletter, Around the World, and wrote a weekly column, Call For News. Additionally, Jim filled the role of webmaster for MAF's Learning Technologies division.

In 2015 he left MAF to pursue writing full-time. He now focuses on aviation and space commentary as well as science fiction novels that reach out to non-believers. Jim continues to serve as a volunteer ferry pilot and writer for MAF Blog Spot.

He and his wife live in Idaho. See his website, www.JRManley.com, for current posts and projects.

www.ingramcontent.com/pod-product-compliance
Lightning Source LLC
Chambersburg PA
CBHW031513040426
42445CB00009B/204